An American Girlhood

Mary Lou Sailor, 1946

An American Girlhood

1924 ♥ 1947

Mary Lou Walbridge

Edited by
John Walbridge III
and
Mary Walbridge Vandeveld

Published by

The Ramsay Press

Bloomington, Indiana

Copyright © 2011 Mary Lou Walbridge

All rights reserved.

ISBN:0615552188
ISBN-13:9780615552187

DEDICATION

With love,
I dedicate this story to my husband
of almost fifty years,
my business partner,
my lover,
and my best friend.

Contents

	Foreword	ix
1	Childhood	1
2	High School	15
3	The Summer of '42	27
4	Washington and Allegheny	31
5	The Summer of '43	43
6	Syracuse	49
7	Christmas of '44	57
8	Postscript on Jim	63
9	The Summer of '45	67
10	Graduation	75
11	A Belle of Washington	81
12	John Walbridge Arrives	89
13	Engaged!	103
14	The Wedding	107
15	The Honeymoon	115
	Epilogue: The Next Sixty-Four Years	121
	Appendix: A Sixtieth Anniversary Toast	125

FOREWORD

THIS is not the story of "John begat Mary. Mary begat John." All that is available in our library up to the most recent begettings. This is the story of a young girl growing to womanhood in a very interesting period of history.

However, this is not a story of history either. It is the story of me as a person at a time when you did not know me—or, at least, you did not know me in the early parts of this tale. I would like to have you know me another way than as Mother, Grandmother, and some day Great-Grandmother, as I wish I could have known my ancestors.

So here I am, for better or for worse—often for worse, as most human beings are.

Mary Lou, 1925

Chapter One

Childhood

JANUARY 1st, 1918, WAS A LUCKY DAY for me. My parents eloped to Little Rock, Arkansas—by train. Dad had just graduated from the University of Arkansas where he belonged to the forerunner of the ROTC. Their unit had been called out, and he was on his way to Camp Pike in Little Rock to prepare to go overseas to help the Allied effort in World War I. He wanted to be a machine gunner but eventually was put in the Intelligence Corps.

My father, Vance Laird Sailor, aged twenty-three at the time of the elopement, had a distinguished career at the University of Arkansas. He started off with a major in music —piano to be precise—but he soon switched to business. He was editor of the yearbook and was the rascal, along with some of his fellow journalists, who changed the name from *The Cardinal* to *The Razorback*. They were almost thrown out of school for doing this, but, as you probably know, that mean-looking pig became an instant hit with the student body and general public. At some future time, all the sports teams were renamed the Razorbacks. I have one or two of his *Razorback* yearbooks in our library. All of these accomplishments did not endear him to my maternal grandfather, Arthur Thompson Lewis, who was an autocratic tyrant to his five

Vance Sailor

daughters. Poor Mother was the oldest, so she suffered through the Methodist ban on card playing, dancing, sewing on Sunday, swearing, alcoholic beverages, and any more than limited contact with young men. As each daughter came along, the rough edges were worn off my grandfather's discipline, until the youngest, Aunt Virginia, eighteen years my mother's junior, became a true flapper and did exactly as she pleased.

My mother, Madge Emily Lewis, aged twenty, was a pretty blonde who happily quit college in the middle of her junior year to marry my father. After the deed was done, she called my grandfather and told him she was married. He forgave her shortly thereafter. When Dad went overseas, she returned home and lived with her parents for the duration. Her contributions to the war effort were rolling bandages and singing at war bond rallies. "Keep the Home Fires Burning" and "Over There" were two of her specialties.

Dad was one of three young officers who decoded messages between the Allies and the German High Command for General Pershing at the railroad car headquarters in France, resulting in the Armistice finalized on November

11th, 1918. Dad wrote a story about this that he unsuccessfully submitted to *Reader's Digest*. It is in our library.

After the Armistice, he was in Germany for a period of time as part of the Army of Occupation. He brought home two future family heirlooms from Europe. One is a green cameo set in etched gold, which he bought from a family he was billeted with in Coblenz. It was a treasure of theirs, but people were very poor after the war and were selling what they could to buy food. The second was the very large Irish linen tablecloth with twelve yard-square napkins woven in a shamrock pattern that he bought on a visit to Ireland. That also was not new when he bought it, so sometime around the year 2000, it had its hundredth birthday. It was used by Mother, and later by me, for family feasts such as Easter, Thanksgiving, and Christmas.

When Dad returned from World War I, my Grandfather Lewis wanted him to go into his bank and understudy him, to become president eventually. My father would not do this, as he felt he

Madge Emily Lewis

Lewis, Mary Lou, and Madge

would be taking charity from his father-in-law. Thus, he went to work as a national bank examiner, moving hither and yon over the next few years. My brother, Vance Lewis Sailor, was born on June 28th, 1920, in Springfield, Missouri. Then the family moved to St. Louis, where they lived on Adams Road in the suburb of Kirkwood long enough for me, Mary Lou Sailor, to be born on

November 18th, 1924, in St. Luke's Hospital. I was born with brown eyes, which is my only claim to fame. Even little black babies are born with blue eyes. My brother was the first grandson, on both sides of the family, and I was the first granddaughter. He was born with all four grandparents and all eight great-grandparents living. By the time I came along, one great-grandparent, Great-Grandfather Sailor, had died. This is rather remarkable since our parents were in their mid-twenties when we were born.

We then moved to Little Rock, Arkansas; Fort Smith, Arkansas; and then back to Kirkwood, where I started school at Keysor School on Geyer Road. My conscientious little bookworm tendencies surfaced early, causing me to skip the second half of first grade and the first half of fourth grade, and since I started at midterm, I eventually graduated from high school, all askew, at midterm. However, I did not learn to tie my shoes until I was in fourth grade and never learned the Palmer method of handwriting. I was a very shy child, which created some difficulties for me on occasions. Once, I received the reward of being allowed to wash the little milk bottles that our morning milk came in. This was done in the same room the furnace was in, and it was a great honor to be able to do it. I dropped one of the bottles in the sink and broke it. In trying to pick up the evidence of the "crime," I cut my thumb very badly. I

Jane Claire Brown

still have the scar. Of course, I could not tell the teacher, so I wrapped my thumb in my handkerchief and went back to class. I was filled with remorse, was bleeding profusely, and was in a great deal of pain. When the teacher called on me for something, I stood up and promptly fainted. The dear lady rushed me to the doctor's, where I was stitched up and comforted.

The Lewis house, Fayetteville, 2009

About this time, Dad went into a bank in St. Louis, leaving his first love, bank examining.

When I was four years old, Mother's sister Claire died of a ruptured appendix, leaving her two-year-old daughter motherless. Jane Claire came to live with us until her father could care for her again. She became the sister I did not have—which at the time was a bit of a mixed blessing, as I was not very proficient at sharing. We soon became "Mary Lou 'n' Jane" in the family; and each of us found our niche in our relationship with each other, including our colors. Jane wore blue, green and lavender. I wore red, pink, and yellow. She received blonde dolls for Christmas, and I received brunettes. Jane was very blonde and slightly plump. I was dark and skinny. We each coveted each other's colors and possessions but somehow survived this terrible typecasting and became inseparable companions. After Jane returned to her father and "wicked" stepmother at the age of six, she still spent every summer with us, both of us usually going to our maternal grandparents in Fayetteville, Arkansas. I should qualify the "wicked stepmother." Aunt Wilma was simply not compatible with a rather stubborn little girl who had been moved from pillar to post at the time she needed lots of love. Wilma had no children of her own and, bluntly, was not a good mother to Jane.

Papa E was the oldest of five brothers, each of whom he started in business. They all lived within two blocks of each other, along with numerous second cousins, cousins twice removed, and all of those obscure Southern relations. When we performed a play, they all came to watch and applaud.

Mary Lou, two cousins, and Jane, Fayetteville, 1935

Anyway, Jane and I grew up together in a rather gentle southern way. Our grandparents had a typical Victorian house with a wonderful red glass window, which we spent a lot of time looking out of, seeing the world as a rosy place. Our grandmother was a wonderful cook and a terrible housekeeper, which made life in her house very pleasant. We turned the furniture in the sitting room upside down and made houses, spread our paper dolls all over the floor and wrote and performed plays at least once a year.

Aunt Louise played the background music on the piano. Mama E, as we called our grandmother, had marvelous junk. There were window seats full of old draperies and clothes, from which we designed and made costumes with the help of our two youngest aunts, Louise and Virginia.

Jane and I and our second cousin, Little Herbert, so called because his father was Big Herbert, were a trio in several family weddings—in which naturally I wore pink or yellow, and Jane blue or green. Little Herbert was the ring bearer and usually wore white satin like a little boy named Little Herbert should wear.

A side note on Big Herbert. He decided to run for sheriff and won. He started his eventual fortune by feeding the prisoners milk gravy and bread, using the major part of the food allotment to buy property along the future banks of the Lake of the Ozarks. He eventually became president of Papa E's bank, which assured his more than comfortable position in life.

In the evenings, the brothers and wives came to sit on our front porch, bringing their visiting grandchildren. We played sidewalk games and caught lightning bugs, for which Mama E supplied canning jars. The porch swing squeaked, and the wicker rockers creaked while they compared notes on the state of the farms and businesses in the county. My grandparents never went to sit on the brothers' porches, as he was the patriarch. On Saturday afternoons, we went to the cemetery to put flowers on the family graves, including Jane's mother's. We played around the cemetery, reading the gravestones. Graves of children were our favorites. We shivered and wondered what had killed them at such a tender age. We were taught never to step on a grave. That was a terrible sin.

On Saturday nights, we went to town to walk around the town square and visit each store, including the marvelous "hardware"

CHILDHOOD

Lewis Bros. Hardware, 2009
Now a bank

store that my grandfather had helped his younger brothers to start. It sold harnesses, tools, nails, Havilland china, furniture, and all manner of fascinating things. Our reward for virtue was a frozen custard ice cream cone from Steve the Greek's stand—but, of course, we were always virtuous. We never disobeyed our grandparents. On weekend afternoons, Jane, Little Herbert, and I often went out to visit one of the farms that Pape E and Uncle Bert, his next brother, owned. We herded the calves up and down the corral, chased the chickens, and, once in a while, got to wade in the creek that meandered through their biggest farm. We always came home with bushel baskets full of peaches, luscious purple Concord grapes, apples, or boxes of fresh brown eggs, which most young people have never seen today.

My grandmother did all the cooking with the big meal served at noon in the summer dining room, which was a screened-in back porch. There was always Jell-O, iced tea, and boiled custard. We were allowed to drink all the tea we wanted, but never coffee. That would stunt our growth. Years earlier, Papa E had visited the Kellogg Clinic in Battle Creek, Michigan, which was affiliated with the Kellogg Company. They determined that he had an ulcer and prescribed a very strange diet for him, which consisted mostly of Kellogg Bran Flakes. He sat at the head of the table with his bowl of bran flakes, serving us fried chicken with mashed potatoes laced with real butter and cream and assorted vegetables cooked with lots of butter or bacon fat. He would comment on how good something looked and would pile it into his cereal bowl on top of his bran flakes. Dinner would end with either homemade ice cream that we children had turned by hand, or a delicious fruit cobbler, made from fresh fruit with a tender lard crust. Of course, this also went on top of Papa E's bran flakes. After dinner, he napped on the blue plush sofa in the sitting room with a handkerchief over his face. At that point, we children did not stir for fear of waking Papa E.

I should tell you something about my aunts, Mother's younger sisters. Aunt Claire, Jane's mother, was Mother's next sister. She had an artistic bent and a Bohemian temperament to go with it. She was the only daughter to escape to a college out of town. She went to Cottey College in Nevada, Missouri, for a year, before returning to the University of Arkansas where she met Uncle Jimmy. She was the daughter who did outrageous things. Once she hennaed her blond hair, which was supposed to become red, which would have been bad enough, as far as "Papa" was concerned. Unfortunately, it turned greenish red. She was banished from the dinner table until it grew out. She painted china in the mode of the day. She died at age twenty-nine, leaving her daugh-

CHILDHOOD

Jane and Mary Lou, 1937

ter Jane Claire. Jane and her husband later named their first child, born in Japan, Claire Lewis, after her grandmother. Tragically, the baby died when she was five days old of a heart defect. She is buried next to her grandmother in Fayetteville.

Aunt Betty, the aunt I was always closest to, graduated from the University of Arkansas, having learned business skills, so she was able to escape to Chicago to live where she met her future husband, Harmon.

Louise and Virginia were the two baby sisters, fourteen and sixteen years younger than Mother. Louise was a talented pianist who could improvise any tune. All of the sisters were pretty except Louise, but she seemed to make up for it with her very outgoing personality. She studied business at the University of Arkansas and then went to work for "Papa" at the bank. Jane and I called her "Aunt Pitty Pat," after the maiden lady in *Gone with the Wind*, as she was still not married at the age of twenty-eight. She surprised everyone by marrying at twenty-nine and then, when her first husband was killed in an auto accident, leaving her with three little girls, captured a charming second husband. So much for homely ladies.

Virginia, only eleven years older than I, was the flapper. She wore short skirts, danced the Charleston, and had dozens of boyfriends. A student she was not! She went to the university expressly to join Chi Omega and to fraternize with the boys in the frats. She had one boyfriend who worked part time in an Eskimo Pie factory—those luscious little chocolate-covered ice cream bars. When he came to see her, he brought us bags of broken Eskimo Pies that they could not sell. She had another boyfriend who had a car with a rumble seat. He very generously took Jane and me for frequent rides. Eventually, her rather carefree ways caught up with her, and she found herself pregnant. My father saved the day as the chief counselor and negotiator, and she and Uncle Horace were married in plenty of time to be the legal parents of their first child. She moved to Little Rock, leaving college without shedding a tear, and became a very proper matron and member of the Junior League of Little Rock. She recently had her eightieth birthday and can claim the distinction of belonging to the same country club as President Clinton. So much for sin.

Mama E also had difficulty throwing anything away. She had a marvelous sleeping porch full of ancient Sears catalogues, *Ladies' Home Journals, Good Housekeeping*, and obsolete patterns ad infinitum. Jane and I were often relegated to that porch to sleep, and it was very spooky at night with its piles of dusty magazines. Later, when my grandmother was ill in a nursing home, my poor mother and her sisters had to wade through this eclectic collection of junk.

At the end of each summer, Jane and I parted with tears, and we each went back to our own households, hers in Memphis and later Montgomery, Alabama, and mine usually in Kirkwood.

During the period we spent in Louisville, we acquired a black maid named Mary. When we returned to St. Louis to live, Mother asked Mary to come with us. She came briefly and then substituted her mother, Ila Mae, who worked for us for most of the years I was growing up. Thus, I did not learn to cook, mend, iron or do any of the useful things that young ladies should be taught. Ila Mae was a master of biscuits, fried chicken, pies of all sorts, and about any other aspect of good Southern cooking—all made with either butter or lard. She came each morning to fix breakfast for my father before he took the commuter train to St. Louis. My father and I remained skinny, which Mother said was our nature, while Mother stayed nicely round.

When I was thirteen, I was allowed to go into St. Louis on the streetcar or train with my girlfriends. We did what kids do today—went to the big downtown movie theaters, tried on clothes in the department stores (there were no malls), and window-shopped. It was a very carefree life without too many rules. This

Ila Mae and Pat

made it very difficult for me later when I went to a strict college. We rode our bikes out into the country where my friend Dottie

Wolf and I took up spelunking, which I did not tell my mother about. There were lots of deposits of limestone around the area with interesting caves you could wiggle into on your stomach. We also "mountain climbed" in the limestone quarries. How could I have done that?!

Dottie's father was an emigration attorney, and her mother was a Quaker. I loved to spend the night with them. They were the people who made me a liberal. Their dinner conversation was part of my education, and I will always be grateful to them. On the other hand, she had an older sister, Margaret, who was always telling us to stand up straight, not to bite our fingernails, to wash our faces with great vigor or we would get acne, etc., etc., ad nauseam. I saw her fifty years later when she took John and me on a tour of the revitalized downtown St. Louis and had us to her exquisite apartment. We found her a thoroughly delightful person. Which one of us had changed, or could it be both?

♥

Chapter Two

High School

NOW BACK to my linear history. When the crash came in the later twenties and early thirties, my father's bank closed. He was fortunate to be able to go back to bank examining when many people were without jobs. Dad got a job helping to organize the examining system of the Federal Deposit Insurance Corporation. In the summer of 1933, our family went to Washington to spend the summer while Dad worked with the task force. There was no dreadful "Beltway." The citizens owned the city; and we, with another FDIC family, spent our summer sightseeing.

We sat in the Chief Justice's seat in the Supreme Court, rode the underground railway from the Senate office building to the Capitol, toured the White House, and went through Mount Vernon before the rooms were roped off. The muggers, purse snatchers, dope pushers, and bombers had not yet arrived on the scene. After that summer, our family went to Frankfort, Kentucky, for a temporary assignment to start examining the banks to set up the new insurance system. Dad's office was in the capitol. We lived in a duplex across the street, which still stands. Dozens of typists were in a huge marble room with high ceilings, pounding out eight carbon copies of every examiner's report. It was deafening. Our dog, Pat, played with the governor's dog on the other side of the capitol. Brother Lewis and I played a game when Dad worked late in his capitol office. We would let Pat loose on the top floor of the capitol, count to one hundred, and then pursue Pat, who took off lickety-split down the stairs. The first one to find him won the game. We were two of the few children to have a marble playhouse. I "studied" at home those few months with books from Keysor School in Kirkwood.

Vance Sailor, Bank Examiner, 1941

Next we moved for a year to Louisville, Kentucky, where the district headquarters was set up. I hated the school there, and all I can recall about it was throwing up in school several times. By then, I was a very frail child. I suspect I had undiagnosed rheumatic fever. There was not much you could do about it anyway if it was diagnosed, as antibiotics had not been discovered. Mother stuffed me with milk shakes, homemade beef broth, hot chocolate, and anything else I would eat.

Eventually we returned to Kirkwood when the FDIC district office for Missouri and several other Midwest states was set up there. We moved to the house on Pitman Place. we were to rent until I graduated from high school We did not buy a house because at that time bank examiners could not get loans from banks they examined. I entered sixth grade there at Adams Middle School and then progressed to junior and senior high school.

My introduction to social life with my peers started in junior high school when our parents sponsored ballroom dancing classes, called "Fortnightly," that we were forced to attend. We wore little taffeta dresses with sashes. I despised the whole routine. I was very skinny, pale, and shy. The girls sat on one side of the room, and the boys on the other. On orders from the teacher, the boys had to ask a girl to dance. This was a very painful thing for someone who was 5'-6" tall and weighed ninety-five pounds. Of course, the ideal woman at that time was Betty Grable, a busty blonde actress whom I did not remotely resemble. Somehow my friends and I survived this awful experience and went on to a "Group" of girls who exchanged parties with a "Group" of boys. This did not involve dates. We all collected records of the big bands and had parties at our homes where we danced to the records, drank cokes, and ate sloppy joes. The worst that happened was that some boy would turn the lights out, bringing our parents dashing down from upstairs to see what we were up to. Usually, it wasn't much.

Meanwhile, back at school, I had this nasty little instinct to do everything perfectly. I was never late for class, always did my homework, and generally ingratiated myself to my teachers by being so utterly good. My friend Margaret was also a good student, and we were the only females who went on to the third year of math. One Friday, our teacher gave us twenty algebra problems that were in our textbook and told us that those problems would be our test on Monday. He said we could take our books home or do whatever we wanted to do. Margaret later became a college math teacher. We hunkered down at her house for the weekend and worked out all twenty problems. The boys goofed off all weekend in typical teenage male fashion. On Monday we all took the test. We females finished about fifteen of the problems in the

Betty Seavers, Mary Lou, Margaret Batts, Junior-Senior Boat Trip, 1940

time allotted while our male rivals, including two future NASA scientists, finished one or two. This really endeared us to those guys. Some were still complaining about it at our fiftieth class reunion.

In spite of doing awful things like that, I did get a boyfriend partway through my junior year. His name was Donald Dickey. He played the piano, tuba, and bass fiddle, two of which he frequently had to carry home from school, with my help. We stuffed our books inside the tuba. Don had other talents. He was a good cartoonist and could imitate Donald Duck perfectly. What more could a girl ask for? He was the older son of a young widowed mother and was reliable, nice, and rather unexciting. However, we did teach each other how to kiss—though he may have already known how, as he was better at it than I was. I remember going to movies with my girlfriends, with all of us studying the love scenes to see what you did with your nose when you kissed someone. I was under no delusion that I was "in love" with Don, but it was nice to have a dependable boy to take me to parties and the movies.

Before leaving my high school years, I should tell you a little about how we dressed. You could probably have picked one of us up out of that era and dropped us down today, and we would not have looked that odd. We wore short pleated or straight skirts, cotton blouses, baggy sweaters, and saddle shoes as a uniform. We made our sweaters on round needles like I still do today, often knitting in the movies. For batting around on our bicycles, we wore boy's jeans, since they did not have girls' jeans then, and our fathers' old white shirts tied in a knot at our waists. Our fathers sometimes objected to losing their shirts to their daughters, so you had to be sneaky about it. Tee shirts, ex

The Boat Trip

Mary Lou and lifeguard George Illich, Lake Bluff, 1941

cept as men's underwear, were unheard of. We wore our hair long and straight or short and curly. I sort of alternated, depending on who influenced me last, be it an admired older girl or a current boyfriend. Besides record parties, in my later years in high school after I acquired Don, we went down to St. Louis occasionally on dates to the movies, a concert, or the amusement park, stopping for hamburgers on the way home or going to the airport to watch planes land and take off. No one drank or smoked. That was taboo for the "in" group. Friday nights were movie nights with your friends of the same sex, but often after the movie we would have a bunking party at someone's house, and the boys would come over and crash the party. We had hayrides with real horses, which were legalized necking parties, and barn dances. After several weeks of practice, we caroled on Christmas Eve to raise money for the Tuberculosis Society, which later became the March of Dimes. We all wound up going to midnight mass at the

BUNDLES FOR BRITAIN Pupils at Kirkwood High school gathered "Bundles for Britain" contributions yesterday. From left, Elizabeth Shanley, Margaret Batts, Ruth Dawson, Doris Dill, Sharlot Williams, Helen Stubbs and Mary Lou Sailor. The collection was made by members of the Pams and Hi-Y clubs. —By a Post-Dispatch Staff Photographer.

Vance in uniform with Mary Lou, 1942

Episcopal church. That was the beginning of my interest in that church. We were Methodists, which was a rather dry, unimaginative religion with lots of "Thou shalt nots"!

In the early summer of 1941, Dad, a major in the army reserves, was called up. Roosevelt had started activating the reservists, since he saw America headed into the war. England was reaching a state of desperation, and my girlfriends and I were busy knitting sweaters for the English children and soldiers. We were also collecting used clothing and packing up "Bundles for Britain." However, the war seemed very unreal to us and, as a matter of fact, rather romantic—like the handsome RAF pilots in the war movies with white silk scarves around their necks and beautiful titled English girlfriends. How naive we were! Dad's entry into the army, with its inevitable disruption of our lives, did shake me up a little. He was temporarily assigned to Fort Leonard Wood in Missouri that summer of 1941, and Mother and I went to visit him and to attend a formal dance at the Officer's Club. This was heady stuff. War was kind of fun! Then, in the fall of 1941, he was sent to Washington, where he was to spend the war in recruiting and induction, mostly for the Women's Army Corps, finishing the war as a full colonel. Mother and I stayed behind to allow me to graduate from high school. I had my seventeenth birthday in November. On December 7th, the Japanese attacked Pearl Harbor, and the United States was at war. I didn't even know where Pearl Harbor was! Immediately, the country went full speed ahead with the war effort. My male classmates were looking at the draft on their eighteenth birthdays. My brother, who was a senior at De Pauw University, majoring in physics, started trying to see his role in the war; and, of course, American industry did the most remarkable job of mobilizing for our defense that had ever been seen.

I graduated in early January 1942. I was valedictorian of my class, a member of the National Honor Society, and won the DAR good citizenship award. However, I felt no great sense of achievement from this. I would rather have been a cheerleader. At that point in my life, like most teenagers, I longed for social acceptance by my peers.

Mother and I packed to move to Washington. First, though, she determined that we should visit all of the family in the Midwest, as we probably would not be back for the duration of the war. I said a very reluctant goodbye to my friends, both male and female. In spite of dancing school and that terrible math test, our little mid-year class of forty-two students was very close. I was not to see most of them again for fifty years and some, never again. Don was half a year behind me in school, so I have never seen him again. In fact, I have difficulty remembering what he looked like. Ah, the fickle heart of a teenager! We did exchange a number of farewell kisses and swore to write to each other, which we never did. His lovely widowed mother had me to dinner before I left. She, Donald, his younger brother, and I sat at her beautiful long mahogany table, eating with sterling silver from her Spode china. That was the first time I had eaten asparagus, which I thought I did not like. All proper young ladies ate everything that was put before them when dining at someone's house, whether they liked it or not. I munched up the hated asparagus and washed it down with gulps from Donald's mother's exquisite French crystal goblets. Now asparagus is my favorite vegetable. Thank you, Donald's mother!

Mother and I toured Fayetteville, Little Rock, and Pittsburg, Kansas, visiting grandparents, aunts, uncles, and cousins, bringing along our little black cocker spaniel, Mosie. Our last stop was to be Lake Bluff, Illinois, where my favorite aunt and uncle, Betty and Harmon, lived. Dad had found an apartment for us in Virginia across the river from Washington, and we were scheduled to go on to Washington after a two-week stay in Lake Bluff. My cousin Jane was already there for the whole summer. As you probably recall, she usually spent each summer with us; but since we were homeless that summer of '42, she went there instead. She was fifteen that year, and I was a sophisticated seventeen. Betty loved having two teenaged girls to help as babysitters and to generally substitute for the daughters she had never had. Her two sons, Harmon Jr. and John, were nine and six years old, so one of our primary duties was to take them to the beach and to babysit with them on occasion in the evening. When my two weeks were up, Jane, Betty, and I begged Mother to let me stay longer. Thus, Mother went off to settle our apartment in Washington with only the company of our little cocker spaniel on the long drive.

I had one little problem to solve. I was enrolled at De Pauw University in Indiana where my much-admired older brother had gone. Mother and Dad decided that was too far for me to travel from Washington, so we had to select another college at a very late time to get in. I applied first to William and Mary, but their freshman class was full. Through a friend of Betty's, I heard of

Allegheny College in Meadville, Pennsylvania. Like De Pauw, it was a small liberal arts coeducational college with a Methodist background. I applied and was accepted, and that problem was resolved. Thus I was free to enjoy my summer of '42, which was the last carefree summer of my life. The war was still very far away from me personally. I was suspended in time for one glorious summer.

The next part of this story is intertwined with my relationships with the four young men who helped shape my emotional development from a young naive girl to a reasonably mature young woman—the years between seventeen and twenty-two, when I married. One, obviously was your father. Two of them tragically died when they were twenty-one. It is also the story of my college years, mostly during wartime, my close and wonderful girlfriends and cousin, my life in the exciting city of wartime Washington, and the tragedies that influenced my life.

♥

Mary Lou, 1942

Chapter Three

The Summer of '42

LAKE BLUFF WAS A SMALL TOWN, the last of the North Shore suburbs of Chicago. For a St. Louis girl, the idea of a beach you could ride your bike to was heaven. Jane and I immediately met two seventeen-year-old boys, and the four of us became inseparable companions for the summer—which, of course, was one of the reasons I did not want to go to Washington with Mother until time to go to college. The nice thing about these boys is that they did not know I was a bookworm. I might even have been a cheerleader as far as they knew. My guy, Brad, was six months younger than I and still had a year of high school to finish. However, even though he looked like a jock and was one, he was very smart, which he did not mention to me either. More about that when I write about my Washington years. The boys had daytime summer jobs working for the village, so during the day we helped Betty in the morning with the chores. It was washing on Monday, ironing on Tuesday, shopping on Wednesday, cleaning the upstairs on

Thursday, and cleaning the downstairs on Friday. When we hung the laundry up, it was all sorted by matching socks, each individual's underwear, and so on ad neatum. Guess who picked up that housekeeping system, which I have diligently been trying to break myself of in my retirement years.

We rushed through the work so we could make tuna fish and egg salad sandwiches and all go to the beach for lunch and the afternoon, working on our tans. We had great fun with Betty, and she with us. When we all came home after our beach time, Jane and I hastily did our hair and helped with dinner so we could spend the evening with our beaus. If one of them got the car, we would go to one of the little roadhouses, where we danced to the juke box and drank cokes. If not, we rode our bikes to the beach. Either way, I soon found out that Brad definitely outclassed Donald in kissing.

On weekends, we rolled Brad's sailing canoe down the hill to the beach on its trailer. It was wood and very heavy. We launched it and sailed it up and down the shores of Lake Michigan, ducking under the boom when we turned. Brad's parents and Jane's beau John Behel's parents were friends of Betty and Harmon's, so sometimes the families had beach picnics together—which, of course, we attended, spending as little time in sight of our elders as possible. That seems to be an eternal trait of teenagers. It was a beautiful summer with the war a million miles away. We four did what teenagers do, which was not as much as they are reputed to do today. Anyway, by the end of the summer, my primary talent was not being a bookworm.

In mid-August, I was ordered to take a train to Washington and start getting ready to go to college. Brad and I parted reluctantly; but once more, as with Donald, I knew this was not real grownup love. Looking back, it was the raging hormones of seventeen-year-olds.

In this tiny village of Lake Bluff lived a young man named John Walbridge. He happened to be in Florida that summer, so our paths never crossed. The following summer when I was in Washington in the midst of my love affair with Jim, which you will hear about later, John Walbridge was in Florida with my old beau Brad, fishing for the summer as a temporary profession. The two of them were living off the land—or rather the sea, as your father likes to describe it. They did not know that they would eventually have something else in common—me! When Uncle Harmon took me to the train to go to my new home in Washington, he heaved a sigh of relief. He had commented shortly before that if he fell over those two boys on his porch once more, he might slit all of our throats! He got a slight overdose of teenagers before his time. Anyway, thank you, Betty and Harmon, for one of the most idyllic summers of my life!

♥

Jim Peete

Chapter Four

Washington and Allegheny

I MET JIM THE FIRST DAY I was in Washington when I was seventeen and he was eighteen. The city was a small town gone crazy with thousands of people coming into the city to manage the war, my father included. Dad was fortunate to find a third-floor apartment with no elevator across the river in Arlington, Virginia. And, of course, air conditioning was rare in 1942. Jim's family had moved there a couple of years before and had luckily gotten a first-floor apartment in another entry off of the courtyard. Mother was a very friendly person, taking to her heart all babies, children, young people, and animals. Thus, by the time I arrived in Washington in late August, Mother had a collection of friends and acquaintances in our apartment complex, including Jim. She met most of these people walking our little cocker spaniel Mosie.

The first morning, when I crawled out of bed on a steamy Virginia day, I was told to walk the dog. As I cut across the courtyard toward a field that looked like a likely dog privy, a tall blonde young man walked up to me. I remember the first words Jim said to me and the last words. The first ones were "You must be Mrs. Sailor's brat, Mary Lou." I cannot remember how I answered that particular opening; but as he helped me walk the dog, he told me he lived in the apartment complex, that he was about to start his second year at Georgetown University, and that he was in the process of trying to get into the Navy V-5 program, the Navy air training unit. The critical problem at the moment was that at 6'-2", he was too tall and had to get a waiver to be in the pilot program. He was nice and very good looking, but I was still under the spell of Brad and my summer of '42, so I was not really in the market for a new swain. I had about two weeks to get ready to go to college, which included getting together my clothes, linens, a wardrobe trunk, and other necessary survival items. I had hung on in Lake Bluff until the last possible moment. I did find that the evenings wore a bit thin, sitting in the hot third-floor apartment with only my mother and father for company, so when Jim asked me to go to a movie, I went. We did a few other minor things together that I cannot recall, and then I had to leave for Allegheny. He seemed like good company, but I really did not have much chance to get to know him.

 The day came that I had to leave for school. I was very scared. I had never been away from home on my own and did not have one single friend waiting for me. I knew Allegheny was a mistake almost from the first day I arrived there. We had selected a school supposedly close to Washington. That was mistake number one. Rail transportation was quite good at that time, but this particular trek required changing trains in the middle of a nine-hour journey. Returning to Washington, you had to change in the middle of the night. But I will tell you more about that later.

 Allegheny was a small coed college with about eleven hundred students located in Meadville, Pennsylvania, which is in the mountains—very cold mountains. I think I got the last room in the ancient freshman dorm, along with my new roommate, Nan Altman. Our room was miniscule, and every pipe—steam, water, and sewer—met in our room, hissing and rumbling all day and all night. We had one large window with no screen, looking down three stories onto a concrete courtyard. Our one closet was a tiny cubbyhole. Nan and I arrived about the same time. We stood looking at each other in this appalling room, sizing each other up

Nan Altman

and wishing we were someplace else. Little hick from Missouri meets Jewish princess from Boston, an actual shirttail relative of the department store clan. With Nan and me, it was love at second sight. I think our dreadful little pad drew us together. At first, we harassed the dean to find us another room. There just wasn't one, so we shifted gears to try to "decorate" it. We shopped for the usual coed bedspreads and draperies and assembled another makeshift closet area, and it was soon home sweet home. Shortly after we moved in, I had a nightmare and started to crawl out the third floor window. Nan woke up in time to grab me by the ankle before I smashed my brains out on the courtyard below. The next morning, a workman arrived to put a heavy screen over the opening.

Nan set about to polish the raw material that had been thrust upon her. She was relieved to find I liked classical music, thanks to my years of going to the symphony and opera in St. Louis in my student days. Missouri to her was the frontier, and she had expected hillbilly tunes. I did not dare to tell her about my Arkansas roots until much later. That was Dogpatch country. She spoke very proper Boston English, was interested in politics, and soon had me tuning into a more "cultural" world. Her next chore was to get rid of my ruffles.

"You are very fortunate to be tall and slim," she said with her Boston twang. "I would give anything to be more than 5' 2". To prove her point, she gave me what turned out to be two of my greatest treasures during the rest of the war when clothing was so scarce—the beautiful princess-style blue wool dress that she had bought at Altman's, that Mecca of fashion, and one of her two pairs of nylon stockings. Nylon and silk had gone to war in parachutes, so we all had to wear baggy rayon stockings. The dress fit because where Nan was round, I was straight.

We worked hard together too. She was a conscientious student, as I was, so we shut our door and studied in the evenings, setting the difficult patterns you have to set for yourself when you are suddenly in an unstructured study environment.

The other girls were great too, though quite different from sophisticated Nan. Most of them were from the environs of Pittsburg, one of the toughest cities in the country at that time, with its roots in the mines and steel mills. I finally got the real sex education that my mother had neglected. I found out what all those words meant that were written on bathroom walls. That was probably fortunate, as I had a definite deficiency in that department when I arrived at Allegheny. The Upper Peninsula was to later complete that part of my education.

I was lucky enough to meet Nan for one major reason. She could not get into most colleges in spite of her excellent academic record. Almost all colleges had quotas on Jews, and some did not admit them at all. It was surreptitious but extremely real. I had never known a Jewish person well. My father had some business contacts who were Jewish, one of whom supplied us with scarce toilet paper and Kleenex all through the war. But they were not people I knew well or identified with. I was soon to get the whole shocking story of what a pretty, bright blonde girl and her charming parents had to put up with in 1942. When they traveled, they had a difficult time finding hotels or motels that they could stay in. "Restricted" was the word on the signs. It meant bluntly, "No Jews." This knowledge added to my liberal views, which had started with the Quaker mother of my high school girlfriend.

I soon settled into the typical liberal arts curriculum of Spanish, English, social studies, and a few other things I cannot recall that were supposed to develop me as a "whole person." The day I went to the college bookstore to buy my books, I received the nickname I was to carry all through college and still have among my old school friends. The cute red-haired young man who handed me my books said, "There you are, Skipper"—which, of course, came from my last name of Sailor. Nan heard it and promptly renamed me Skipper, which later became Skippy. I hated my syrupy sweet Southern name of Mary Lou. In high school I had changed the spelling but nothing helped. I was more than happy to shed that moniker and move into the much more interesting name of Skippy. I suspect that all children, particularly girls, should be allowed to name themselves when they reach the age of reason.

My extracurricular activity became the Children's Theater, which Allegheny put on for the children of Meadville. I was thrilled when I got the part of Raggedy Ann in their first production of the year—I suspect because I was tall and skinny. I remember that on the night of the first performance, the battery that lighted my heart and that was suppose to glow with loving kindness, went dead. The director snatched up my skirt to put a new one in the pack that hung around my waist. I was mortified! But such are the indignities suffered by great actresses.

We were required to go to chapel every day at noon. It was a half hour of announcements, prayers, sermons, and hymn singing, which of course we all hated. Nan was excused because she was Jewish. The dining hall food, for a little Southern girl raised on chicken fried in butter, homemade biscuits, and pecan pie, was dreadful. Food rationing had started and the civilian population got the things the men in the services did not like. Butter went to war, and we had the forerunner of oleomargarine, which tasted like lard and had to be colored by kneading in a little food coloring pellet. Chocolate disappeared. Beef and pork were repaced by lamb, which I had never eaten, and chicken done in some terrible Northern fashion.

I celebrated my eighteenth birthday with a cake Mother sent from home. By the beginning of November, I was very homesick.

Mary Lou's 18th birthday party, Allegheny

WASHINGTON AND ALLEGHENY

I had never been away from home on a major holiday. I begged Mother and Dad to let me come home for Thanksgiving. I suspect they were lonesome for me too, since my brother was now in the Army Air Forces at MIT learning to be a meteorologist. Even though they could not afford it on my father's army pay, they sent me my train ticket to leave on Wednesday afternoon, arriving in Washington on Thanksgiving morning. Two other girls from my area were also going home for the holiday. They lived in Baltimore, but we would be taking the same train. We were to leave Meadville on one train in the afternoon, arriving in Pittsburg around 9:00 in the evening with a two-and-a-half hour layover before we could catch our train to Baltimore and Washington.

After giving each of us the third degree, our parents got the names of the other parents of these sheltered daughters who were leaving the "convent" to come home, with that threatening layover in the wicked city of Pittsburg. One of the fathers had a business associate there whom he called on for help. Much to our aggravation, it was arranged for his secretary to meet our train and look after us until we boarded our second train around midnight. We were eighteen-year-old adults, and this was an insult to our ability to cope. In addition, we had in mind heading for a bar and having a drink because it was off limits at Allegheny. Forbidden fruit! Who can resist? Now our plans were thwarted. We arrived on time and looked for the old witch who was to chaperone us for the next two and a half hours. A pretty, sexy-looking young woman sashayed up to us and announced that she was Nancy, our keeper. Would we like to go to a movie, she yawned. "NO," we chorused. "We want to go to a bar." "Fun!" said Nancy. "There just happens to be one close by." We spent our layover drinking some of those awful, sickly sweet drinks that appeal to novice drinkers. Nancy tipped us off as to what was really jazzy and eventually poured us onto the train. Our alcohol threshold was very low, and we crawled into our berths and headed for home feeling a wee bit queasy. We made it, arriving Thanksgiving morning in our home cities without too much appetite for Thanksgiving dinner.

While I was getting my feet wet at college, Jim was back at Georgetown for his second year, entering the Navy V-5 aviation program. He had spent some of his free time wooing my mother by carrying groceries up her two flights, walking the dog, and other nice things that made her think, "Now here is a really nice, trustworthy young man. Also very reliable, smart, handsome, etc., etc.—perfect for my innocent daughter to go out with." She was a good judge of character because that was the way Jim really was. And he was also a romantic, as I was soon to find out. He called me Thanksgiving Day and asked me to go out the following night, this time on a real date. Naturally, Mother and Dad could not object to my leaving them on my brief visit home. This was such a fine young man, as he had convinced them, which of course was his plan.

Every major hotel in Washington had a nightclub with an orchestra for dancing. They usually had a very small cover charge, and you could spend the whole evening there sipping on one drink. During wartime, you rarely went out to dinner on a date. Food was poor and very expensive in most places, and none of the young men in uniform had much money. You would finish the evening by going to one of the White Castles (the forerunner of fast food) for a hamburger and coffee. And that is what we did that first evening.

On the way home, Jim wanted to show me Great Falls Park on the Virginia side of the Potomac River, which was on a cliff overlooking a series of rapids. We drove into the park; and predictably, no one was there. It was a crisp fall night with a beautiful harvest moon, a perfect setting to switch from wooing the mother to wooing the daughter. Of course, by then, Jim was in uniform, looking great in the navy blue officers' uniform the V5 men wore. I had on my high-heeled pumps and a dress, that obsolete garment that we still had in our wardrobe at that time. We strolled through the park hand in hand. We had progressed that far, even though things moved much slower fifty years ago. He wanted to show me the old hand-carved carousel in the park that sat there in those gentler times, unguarded and unmarred by vandals. Naturally, I had to sit on a horse, which I did sidesaddle because of my skirt. When I couldn't get down, Jim had to lift me off, which gave him the opportunity to kiss me for the first time. That is where our love affair started. It was to last for the next two and a half years. When I came home for Christmas vacation, Jim gave me his Georgetown class ring, and neither of us ever went out with anyone else again as long as he lived.

After the little Thanksgiving respite, I felt better about going back to my friends at Allegheny, but the worst was still to come. In early December, the entire ROTC unit at school was called up, as were many others from college campuses around the country. They were moderately trained, so they could be hustled through basic training and sent out to be cannon fodder. I wonder how many of those bright young men died in the next few months when Hitler and Mussolini were rampaging through Europe. We were no longer a coed college.

The old Rudy Vallee movies about life on a college campus being one big party simply did not seem to be true. Our major entertainment, when they let us off campus, was to walk downtown to a diner and have a piece of wonderful hot homemade blueberry pie. By Christmas, I had decided that Allegheny was not for my free spirit.

When I went home for the holidays, I told Mother and Dad that I was going to transfer someplace, anyplace! I hated the strict rules. We had to be signed in every night by 8:00 PM, except on Friday and Saturday when we could stay out until ten. I hated the compulsory chapel. I hated the freezing cold, ugly dormitory with the huge primitive bathrooms. I had numerous other things on my hate list. I had talked to the dean of women; and after making a halfhearted attempt to talk me into staying, she suggested Syracuse. The former Allegheny president had just gone there the year before to become the chancellor. I should have checked the climate at Syracuse before waging war to be allowed to go there.

Now I should digress slightly and tell you how I was brought up. As the second child, I pretty much did what I wanted to do. I did not have any particular rules about what time I had to get in at night or where I could go, within reason. Dad had been gone during most of my high school years, and I could wind my mother around my little finger, conniving child that I was. Thus, I really resented this step backwards into a prisonlike atmosphere. Mother and Dad caved in and said to set the wheels in motion for me to go to Syracuse the next year.

I enjoyed the rest of Christmas vacation with my new beau, Jim, staying out until my usual 2:00AM, which became my pattern in Washington. I have been resting up from it ever since! Jim and I had fun together. We did not spend all of our time making love in romantic parks. He was the first one to show me Washington, since he had been there longer than I. In the next months and years, we visited all the major landmarks, including the boat trip to Mount Vernon, where you could still walk through the house freely without ropes. We went to the Library of Congress, the Smithsonian, and the National Gallery, watched Congress in session, and became avid zoo goers after my family moved to an apartment across the street from the entrance to the National Zoological Park. Later I gave the same guided tours to your father. Washington was a wonderful city, and we enjoyed it freely.

When I went back to Allegheny after Christmas, I took my first real college final exams. It was a terrifying experience, but I survived.

That is when Jim and I started to write to each other, which we did once or twice a week. Later it was three or four times a week, and finally every day. He is the only man I was ever involved with who liked to write letters and wrote exactly like he talked. Our letters were not simply love letters. They were a chronicle of the times. We wrote about our friends, school, the Navy, the war, and always his damned airplane, which he dearly loved. We kept each other's letters. More about that later.

Easter in 1943 coincided with Passover. It was too short a holiday to go home, so Nan and I accepted an invitation to visit Flo Bernstein, the only other Jewish girl in our freshman class, in Pittsburg. She had a beautiful home and a wonderful warm family who set about stuffing me with all the great Passover delicacies. I particularly liked the matzo, the unleavened bread slathered with unsalted butter. They were reformed Jews, so we went to Temple on Sunday; and I heard one of the greatest Easter sermons I have ever heard from the rabbi of that huge congregation.

As spring approached at Allegheny, I was tapped to join the sophomore honor society, Qwens, the Old English word for Queens. Naturally Nan, who was as good a student I was, was not invited to join, because she was Jewish. Then they started the sorority rushing—once more leaving out Nan. Of course, I was leaving, so I did not accept any invitations to their parties. At last, I took my final exams and got all my applications in to Syracuse and was accepted. The dear dean of women helped me to do all of this. I left my friends with regret and the place with joy. Nan stayed and went on to graduate from Allegheny. After all, it was no more biased that any other place she could go at that time in our history. In spite of my problems at Allegheny, that sneaky little bookworm nature of mine surfaced, and I left with an academic record of all A's.

♥

Jim in his car

Chapter Five

The Summer of '43

MY LUGGAGE AND I ARRIVED back in Washington in May. Naturally my junk had multiplied at Allegheny, but we managed to tuck everything away in our hot little apartment. After greeting my parents and Jim, I went summer job hunting. Jane arrived a few weeks after I did to spend the summer with us, and she joined in the job hunt.

Jim and I had two or three weeks before he was to go to Connecticut to start his flight training. We saw each other almost every night, but I had to reform my hours a bit. I had gotten a job with the British Army Staff in one of their satellite offices: "Movements Registry." We handled the routing of all the freight cars carrying war materials to the harbors for shipment to Europe. I learned to make proper tea for the British officers, and that is when I learned to drink milk and sugar in my tea. I also learned some strange British spellings that I still use occasionally, such as "harbour" instead of "harbor." Jane found a job in another British Army Staff office. We had frequent air raid drills when we all had to go to the basement of our building. Jane's office did not have a basement, so they all dashed across the street to the Mayflower Hotel and sat in the bar. Jane was sixteen, but they always asked her if she wanted a drink—which, of course, she did not. In the District of Columbia, women could be served alcoholic beverages when they were eighteen, but men could not be served until they were twenty-one. No one paid any attention to this. They did have one strict rule, however. A woman could not carry her drink from a bar table to her dinner table; either her male escort or a waiter had to carry it for her. Nor could a woman sit on a bar stool at the bar. She could sit at a table in the bar but not on a barstool. A group of women out by themselves had to act Very Properly, or they would be thrown out. Since Jane and I were the only females we knew, we did not have that problem. We did not hang out in bars.

By the time I was settled in my job, Jim had left for Connecticut. Our big plan of the summer was to meet in New York when he had a weekend pass. Jane and I would save our money for our first visit to the Big Apple, and he would bring a date for her. Somehow we conned my parents into this plan to let a sixteen-year-old and an eighteen-year-old go to the big city by themselves to meet two men. It was not as risqué as it sounded. We were to stay in the Hotel Biltmore where there was a floor for young ladies of college age, supervised by an old dragon who checked you in and out. If you were not in by 2:00 AM, my witching hour, she called your parents or your dean of women, as appropriate. I stayed there several times in the next few years.

Jane and I took the bus each morning from Virginia to our jobs in the District. In Virginia, the black people had to sit in the rear of the bus. In D.C. they could sit anywhere. The buses were not air-conditioned; and each night by the time we got home, we were wilted and exhausted. Every Thursday night, the stores were open until nine, so we stayed downtown to shop and eat a vegetarian dinner at our favorite little cafe. Jane and I were always sufficient unto ourselves, so by the time I left Washington when I married four years later, I did not have a single female friend there. My college friends visited frequently, but I just never had the chance or need to make friends with women.

We almost had a rebellion on the planned trip to New York. On her way to Washington on the train that summer, Jane had met the West Point cadet from Louisiana who was to be her future husband. They were quite smitten with one another and started to write. He invited us to come to West Point for a weekend. We could not afford both trips so had a bit of a disagreement on whose boyfriend would win. Dad settled it by picking Jim, since he knew him.

Duke, Jane, Mary Lou, and Jim
At Duffy's Tavern

Our big weekend finally came, and we took the train to New York. By then it had become highly organized with a bit of graft thrown in. Dad dealt with several big New York advertising agencies. He had become quite friendly with some of the ad execs and asked them if they could get theater tickets for us, as a special treat. They were more than happy to do this for the army officer who bought lots of recruiting advertisements from them; and, what's more, they paid. When we arrived at the Biltmore, we had flowers in our room and a stack of tickets, reservations, and other goodies for us young babes in the big city for the first time. This was before all that stuff was illegal. We saw two plays and went to the Stork Club for dinner. Fortunately, when the boys started to pay the check, they found it was paid for, as it would have taken several months of their pay. We dined the second night at Duffy's Tavern, which was also paid for.

We also did all the usual touristy stuff. I bought a skirt and sweater at Lord and Taylor's. We took a carriage ride in Central Park and went up in the Empire State Building. We made it in on time past the old dragon in the hotel each night and generally had a fairy tale weekend. Jane was not too interested in her date, but I was certainly interested in mine.

After blowing our money, we returned to Washington to get ready to go back to school. Jane was going back for her senior year in high school and I was heading off to Syracuse, another place where I knew no one except the Chancellor, who like me had come from Allegheny. Jane left for home. Jim came home for an end of the summer leave.

Then I left for my new life at Syracuse. Once more I took two trains—but much more "fun" trains. I took the Pennsylvania to Penn Station in New York. It went through Baltimore, Wilmington, Philadelphia, Newark, and then New York. Later as I got acquainted, my girlfriends would board the train along the route, and we would gather in the club car. The train was always full of military men, sometimes whole units and other times lone travelers. A young woman could always get help with her luggage. You also got many invitations to have a drink in the club car or dinner in the diner, but I always refused, as I figured they needed their meager earnings more than I did.

There was one exception to this that I recall. Once I was in a car with a unit of Japanese-American troops on their way to embark for Europe. They were generally well behaved, more so than most units on their way to war; but there was one very obnoxious young man who had tippled a wee bit too much and was pestering me to go to dinner with him. I tried to be polite in refusing him, but he finally started asking me if I thought I was too good to associate with someone with yellow skin. Another young soldier in his unit was watching this with great embarrassment. I was almost in tears, when he stepped forward and said in a very American accent: "Get lost, George. She already promised to go to dinner with me," at which point he escorted me out of the car toward the dining car. As soon as we were out of earshot, he apologized for his friend and said that, of course, he did not expect me to have dinner with him. I told him it would be an honor. That is when I learned about the terrible wrong that we had done to our Japanese-American citizens. It has only recently been acknowledged by Congress. All of the families of these brave young men who later served so gallantly in Europe were incarcerated in concentration camps in California for the duration of the war. They lost their homes, their businesses, and many years of their lives. I hope my Sir Galahad survived the war and had a good life in the country he fought for.

I also met other interesting people on the train. One was Harold Stassen, who was a perennial candidate for President. Another was Gene Kelly, the dancer and movie star. Both were friendly and pleasant, and Gene Kelly even bought me a cup of coffee.

There was a definite dress code for traveling that would seem very strange today. All polite young women wore a dress or suit, a hat, and white gloves. Since you wore hats for a lot of other occasions, you had to carry a large hatbox along with all your other luggage. Once I arrived home without the required hat and gloves, and my mother said to me, "I can't believe that you rode the train that way"—as if I had arrived riding the rods. The Washington to New York part of the trip was the most fun because it was shorter, and you met more interesting people. In New York I had to take a cab or, as I got more experienced, the subway to Grand Central Station to catch the New York Central. After my first journey I arrived at Syracuse, once more ready to cope with a new place and new friends.

♥

The Syracuse Bookworm

Chapter Six

Syracuse

SYRACUSE had approximately seven thousand students in 1943, more than six times as many as Allegheny. I was assigned to a very nice dorm that had been an apartment house. I was in a suite with five other sophomore girls. We even had a washing machine in our basement—the old wringer type—along with clotheslines and an ironing board so I did not have to send my laundry home in a special laundry box for Mother to do, as was the custom at that time. I made a giant step forward during that period. I learned to iron. Ila Mae and Mother had always done my ironing. Spoiled child! I have made up for it over the years.

Sorority rushing started that fall. I joined Tri Delta, partly because Mother had been a Tri Delt and partly because they had an exquisite old house with white pillars, now on the New York State Registry of Historic Buildings. I enrolled in the School of Speech but later added a second major in Psychology. I realized I was not cut out to be a Sara Bernhardt. I loved my speech courses and finally came to the end of my shy period. Though it was not Joe College days at Syracuse either, I liked it there and even tolerated the dreadful winters. Of course, there were few civilian men there. The fraternity houses were closed for the duration.

Army units passed through but did not stay long. I was not shopping for men anyway, as I was committed to Jim. Both of us were home for Christmas in 1943, and then he left for Florida for his advanced flight training when I went back to school. He was in Pensacola first and later Daytona Beach. While I froze that winter with a national coal shortage, he sent me pictures of him and his buddies lounging on the beach.

Tri-Delts, 1943

I moved into the Tri Delt house after Christmas and became part of the tight knit group of twenty-four girls who clung together during the bleak wartime years. We had a most unusual sleeping arrangement that must have come from some ancient tubercular alumna. We all slept in two large unheated rooms on the third floor with the windows open day and night, winter and summer. We had little iron cots lined up side by side, twelve of us in each room. Some nights we slept in ski pants, hats, and mittens, but no one ever thought to close the windows. Our rooms were studies with studio couches, which you could sleep on for a night or two if you had double pneumonia. Like all college women in those days, I signed out when I went out at night and signed in when I came back. We had to be in by ten on weeknights and midnight on Fridays and Saturdays, except for special occasions or proms—which we did not have in those war years. The housemother guarded our virtue from her room at the head of the stairs. Of course, we had a rear fire escape, which was used on occasions with collusion from someone inside the house who would open the second floor fire door. Sneaking in was not really a mortal sin, as Syracuse was a wee bit more liberal and sophisticated than my last prison. Our food was as good as could be expected with rationing. We had a roast every Sunday, and it was usually lamb. That is when I finally learned to eat lamb, which is now my favorite meat. We were always hungry, probably because of the low protein diet. The cook firmly padlocked the refrigerator every night against marauding coeds. Our only snack was peanut butter and jelly and squishy white bread, which I certainly ate my share of.

My roommates that first year in the Tri Delt house were very pretty blonde twin sisters whose approach to dressing was to dig through their dirty clothes and wash what they needed to wear the next day. They often failed to do this in time, and so they helped themselves to my sparse wardrobe. Once, Carol borrowed my beautiful black Chesterfield with the velvet lapels, which I had worked half the summer to buy; and when her date's car got stuck, she obligingly gave him my coat in a Sir Walter Raleigh-type gesture to put under the wheel of the car. She did have it cleaned for me. I was soon shopping around for my next year's roommate, who turned out to be my lifelong friend, Gloria Mitchell Lagergren, who was also shopping for a change.

Life on campus soon settled down to a routine of study and sorority activities. We had several events each year that the university tried to keep up to make some semblance of normal college life. One was step-singing, where the sororities and dormitories competed against each other on the chapel steps for a coveted cup. The Tri Delts were notorious for having awful voices.

However, we had a talented music student, who was later to head the music activities of a large school system and who taught the Tri Delts to sing. We won first prize for two years in a row. Another activity was Class Day, when we put on skits on an assigned theme. I became our official skit writer. My script called "The Brave New World," set in the year 2000, won first place one year. The star of my script was an architectural student who scooted around on a kiddy car, which was supposed to be a spaceship.

I had no idea what I was going to do when I graduated. No one seemed to direct women toward careers that they were capable of. I had vague plans to go into "personnel." The men were urged toward medicine, law, accounting, and other interesting and lucrative fields, but few women had the guts to get into a male field. Thus we were all proud of Catherine Warren, my skit star, for going into architecture.

I received an allowance of ten dollars per month. The money I earned in the summer went for my clothes, my transportation, and a little toward my books. When I started college, my tuition, room, and board were about a thousand dollars a year. By the time I finished, they were almost twelve hundred dollars. I charged my books and study equipment at the bookstore, and my father paid the bill. My huge sum of ten dollars went for necessities like toothpaste, shampoo, and recreation. One of my main recreations was eating an awful concoction called a Virginia Special, which consisted of dry chocolate cake with ice cream and fudge sauce on it. Any self-respecting Virginia cook would have bombed the little store that served it for inserting "Virginia" in its name. I also bought cigarettes, although Jim sent them to me from the Navy commissary, as did Dad from the Army PX. I had worked very hard to learn to smoke when I went to college. By my sophomore year, I was hooked and I survived on the usual exam diet of coffee and cigarettes. I did learn one useful skill, bridge. When we weren't studying, bridge games went on all

SYRACUSE

Gloria Mitchell Lagergren

night. We also listened to the radio each day, anxious for our brothers, friends, and sweethearts off fighting the war.

Syracuse had an excellent School of Fine Arts, and Tri Delta had a goodly number of art students living in the house. They all had to take a basic anatomy course where they drew arms, legs, and other assorted parts from professional nude models. Along with the finished paintings that they hung for their final exams, they had to have their sketchbooks full of little partial drawings of body parts. Toward the end of each semester, they usually found themselves a number of pages short in their sketchbook, so they would con innocent liberal arts students studying for their exams into removing parts of their clothing so they could catch up. A half-nude Tri Delt would attract a large group of fine artists, who would surround her, moving her arms and legs around while they furiously sketched. We models would make them promise not to reveal whose derriere was exposed in their work. One senior Tri Delt student did a portrait of me that I bought from her and gave to my parents for a Christmas present in 1944. It now hangs over our piano.

The summer of 1944 was about like the summer of 1943, except that Jane stayed in Memphis that year, and we missed our usual summer together. It was very lonesome for me. Jim was home at the beginning of the summer but went back to Florida after a two-week leave. Washington was full of unattached men, but I was very faithful and would not go out with anyone—much to the chagrin of my mother, who thought I was too young to be so serious about one man. I did have one male pal—Bill Pollard, whose parents were friends of my parents. He was at George Washington University finishing up pre-med. He took me to parties there occasionally, where I once ran into Margaret Truman, whose father was then Vice President.

In mid-September I went back for my junior year, the first time I had gone to college where friends were waiting for me. My chosen roommate, Gloria Mitchell, was a pretty blonde girl from New Jersey whose mother was English and whose father was Scottish. He worked as a salesman for a meat packing company.

SYRACUSE

Gloria's mother had come to this country as a teenager and had married her father here and then gone back to England for Gloria's birth, so she would be a British citizen. Thus, every year Gloria had to register at the post office as an alien, which annoyed her no end. I often visited Gloria in route to and from school; and her father, with his connections, would always have luscious roast beefs and steaks in my honor.

♥

Jim

Chapter Seven

Christmas of '44

Christmas 1944 was to be Jim's last leave before going off to sea on an aircraft carrier for what would probably be the duration of the war. We had no idea how long that would be. The atomic bomb had not yet been heard of. Since D-Day, we had made good progress in Europe, but that was still an unknown. Thus, it was a bittersweet reunion for us. We had not seen each other for more than six months. Our only contact had been our steady stream of letters. You did not make frivolous phone calls in those war years. He did not have easy access to a phone, and our sorority house had only one line, which you were not allowed to be on for very long, even if you happened to be home when a call came for you.

Jim had his twenty-first birthday in early December and also received his commission as an ensign in the Navy and his coveted wings. How can I describe Jim? At twenty-one, he had turned into a really gorgeous guy—and one of the nice things about him was that he was not particularly aware of it. He was no longer the skinny kid I had first met. Two and a half years and Navy phys-ed training had put on twenty-five pounds. Like his mother, he was a true blonde with those azure blue eyes. His hair was bleached blonde and he was very tan from the Florida sun. He was a late child. His mother was in her forties when he was born; and like me, his parents doted on him and pretty much had always given him free rein.

He had an older brother, whom I did not meet until the following summer. He was in the Army Dental Corps at one of the southern ports of embarkation. He did not resemble Jim at all in appearance or personality. Jim had a happy-go-lucky cheerful disposition, which I have heard is the ideal temperament for a fighter pilot. We never had a major disagreement because he would always tease me out of it if I were provoked. And, realistically, we never had the stress that you have in marriage—children, finances, and other things that can fracture a relationship. We were wartime lovers with the flame fanned by constant separations and reunions.

The first night he was home, he came to pick me up. My father and mother were very fond of Jim, so they made a big fuss over his getting his commission and his Navy wings. He shook my father's hand and kissed my mother, but he certainly was not going to kiss me for the first time in six months in front of my parents. We finally escaped to his car—which was, as usual, parked in the loading zone in front of our apartment that said "No Parking." The nice black night doorman always watched it for him and made excuses to any policeman who came along.

That is where he finally kissed me, with cars honking enthusiastically at us as they drove by. That night he gave me a little gold and pearl ring of his mother's and his Navy wings. I had to give his wings back after he pinned them on me, as it was not legal to give the official ones away. Instead, I got a miniature pair that the Navy provided for that purpose. We almost went off and got married, but I was the practical one. I was only partway through my junior year at Syracuse, and I thought I would have to help him get through college when the war was over, so we didn't do it. By then, he was twenty-one and I was twenty; and after two and a half years, we were very much in love. Ironically, it never occurred to us to ask our parents what they thought about our getting married. I don't think they would have disapproved. I think my father would have continued to send me to college just as his father-in-law had looked after my twenty-year-old mother during World War I. But we did not ask. We went back to our original plan to marry after I graduated as soon as the war was over. We also had a firm understanding that we would not have sex before marriage. That was just not an option "nice" girls considered, war or no war. First, it was immoral according to our strict Protestant upbringing. Then there was fear of pregnancy in the days before the pill. Your mother told you horror stories about girls who "got in trouble."

As with so many of my memories, those two weeks come back to me with music. We walked the streets of downtown Washington, shopping for gifts for our parents. Jim bought me a little stuffed white yarn poodle with a basket of flowers in its mouth since I could not have a real live dog in our apartment. That was the last gift he gave to me. We listened to the Salvation Army brass bands play carols and the canned Christmas music—"Silver Bells, it's Christmas time in the city," one of the few songs that talks about things like city sidewalks, where there is certainly Christmas too. We visited the zoo to check up on the babies born since we had last been there. And we stayed out until our usual 2:00 AM every night except for Christmas, which we each spent with our families. We were happy and invincible, that lorelei of emotions that seduces the young into going to war.

The last night of his leave, I must have had a premonition that something was going to happen. We had said goodbye so many times in our relationship that I was accustomed to it. We had the typical optimism of youth: It can't happen to us. Our life lies ahead of us. But this time was different. We went to our favorite little piano bar up the avenue from my apartment. We sat there holding hands and listening to the haunting songs of wartime that were all about separation, death, and other gloomy themes—"I'll be seeing you in all the old familiar places. I'll see you in the morning sun and when the moon is new." I started to cry. We could not sit there with tears running down my cheeks, so we drove into Rock Creek Park and spent the rest of the evening with my salty tears mixed with our farewell kisses. Finally, we had to go home. Jim was leaving for Florida early in the morning.

Of all nights, Mother waited up for me. She had never done this before, but she wanted to tell Jim goodbye and wish him well. When she heard the elevator stop, she came to the door in her bathrobe. The hall, as usual, was dimly lit since all the eastern cities were at least partially blacked out. After crying all night, I looked rather disheveled, and my long hair was all over Jim's uniform. Jim kissed my mother goodbye and then kissed me for the first time in front of a parent with a kiss that was supposed to last until the end of the war. Then he whispered the last words I ever heard him say. "Goodbye, Sweetheart. I love you." He turned and ran down the four flights of stairs. Mother and I walked into the apartment, and both of us cried. I am sure she remembered that she had eloped with my father at the beginning of World War I when she was twenty.

After the Christmas of 1944, Jim and I wrote each other every day. It was the last thing each of us did before we went to bed. Fortunately, it was the era of the three-cent stamp. Meanwhile, I settled into finishing my junior year. I was really into my psychology courses and took one course from a slightly kooky professor who experimented with hypnosis. I was fascinated. However, I did not turn out to be a good hypnotic subject, much to my disappointment. I did learn how to do it and later hypnotized your father several times, once to get him to concentrate on studying for a boring exam. He got a good grade too. We continued our nun-like existence at the Tri Delt house, eating our peanut butter and jelly sandwiches and playing bridge for recreation.

During my first year at Syracuse, I had taken a Red Cross course to become a Gray Lady, which was a hospital helper. That was my major outside interest, which I continued all through school and again in Washington, the year after I graduated. At Syracuse I worked in the maternity section of the hospital, a forerunner of my daughter's career. The first day I went in there wearing my new uniforms, I got to spend the afternoon emptying bedpans. That was the era when women did not get out of bed for days after they gave birth. Then I was promoted to changing diapers in the nursery. I was so good at that chore that it was the duty I was usually assigned to. I worked two afternoons a week, and it gave me great satisfaction. There was a severe nursing shortage; the nurses had gone to war too. I also got to eat any uneaten dinner trays. They had better food than we had; and, as I told you, we were always hungry.

Mary Lou, the Gray Lady

Early on the evening of April fourth, my father called. He told me that Jim's father had just called to tell us that Jim had been killed. His plane and another had collided out over the Atlantic while practicing formation machine gun strafing. They had crashed into the ocean about fifteen miles off of Daytona Beach. Their bodies were never to be recovered. I cannot described the total shock those words left on a twenty-year-old girl—a girl who had never known anyone close to her who had died. Death was for old people, not for the person you loved most. I cannot remember much about the next few days. I wanted to kill myself, but I did not know how. I had nightmares about the fish nibbling on his body. The girls tried to help me, but they had no concept of what it was like to lose someone so suddenly and violently. I suspect some of them even thought it was a bit romantic—like a tragic novel. Gloria did her best, but I knew that she never had felt that Jim was right for me because of his chosen profession. After a few days, the housemother took me aside and told me that if I did not pull myself together, she was going to send me home. That is the last place I wanted to go. I did not want to see the places that Jim and I had been together or face my parents.

I have always had a lot of moral stamina. I went back to class and operated with one side of my brain while I mourned Jim with the other. Then about two weeks after he died, I had an otherworldly experience that I have never told anyone about and that helped me to start coping with his death. I would always love Jim and he would always be a part of me, but I knew that my life was not meant to be over yet. When Jim died, my girlhood died. I finally knew what war really was.

If I had married Jim, I know I would have had a hard life. I believe he would have stayed in the Navy. He loved the Navy, and he loved flying. If he had survived World War II, he would have been young enough to be in the Korean War. Besides the ever-gnawing worry, I would have been often alone, coping with all the problems you share in a good marriage. But our love affair will always be a little treasure in my heart. Around the anniversary of his death, or sometimes when I catch a glimpse of a tall blonde young man, I once more feel the terrible pain of that call and I stop and pray that he may be in Paradise.

♥

Chapter Eight

Postscript on Jim

As the fiftieth anniversary of Jim's death approached, I began to wonder once more if they had eventually recovered his plane and his body. After the meetings with Jim's mother and brother in the summer of 1945 that I will tell you about in the next chapter, I lost track of his family. I did not even know if they finally had a memorial service for him. I decided I would try to locate his brother—if he was still alive. It was incredibly easy to find him after almost fifty years. Their family had come from Detroit, and David was a dentist. I started by writing to the University of Detroit dental school alumni office. I told them briefly why I was looking for Dr. Peete and asked them to forward my letter to him if they could not give out his address. I did not hear anything for about two weeks; and then a man who sounded very concerned called me from Northwestern Dental School and apologized for taking so long to get back to me. Detroit had forwarded my letter to their office.

He told me he had just called Dr. Peete, and he had no objections to their giving me his address and phone numbers. I promptly wrote David a rather emotional letter reviewing Jim's and my relationship for the benefit of his wife and asked him

2 D. C. Area Air Trainees Die in Crash

Two Washington area men, both student officers of the naval air station at Daytona Beach, Fla., were killed Wednesday afternoon in a crash while practicing strafing 10 miles off the Florida coast, the Navy announced yesterday.

They were Ensign James O. Kowalski, 20, USNR, son of Mr. and Mrs. Oswald J. Kowalski, 4704 Southern ave. se.; and Ensign James C. Peete, 21, USNR, son of Mr. and Mrs. David Peete, 3111 N. 20th st., Arlington, Va.

Naval authorities notified the parents of both men last night that portions of the wrecked planes had

Ensign Peete Ensign Kowalski

been found, but that the bodies had not yet been recovered and that the search would continue today.

Ensign Kowalski, a native of St. Joseph, Mich., was a graduate of St. Paul's High School here. He entered the Navy in May, 1943. His father, who brought his family here in October, 1941, is employed at the Government Printing Office. Besides his parents, Ensign Kowalski leaves two sisters, the Misses Jean and Evelyn Kowalski, both of Washington.

Ensign Peete entered the Navy in June, 1943, and was commissioned last December 15. Since then he had been stationed at Daytona Beach in training as a fighter pilot. Besides his parents he leaves a brother, Lieut. David Peete, jr., with the Army Dental Corps, now stationed at Camp Livingston, La.

---

those things that I wanted to know. His letter to me follows. I now vaguely recall Jim talking about Jimmy Doolittle but I wasn't really into aviation greats at that time and so had forgotten that part. I think you will find his letter interesting, and it was very helpful in settling for me finally Jim's life and death. When we go to Florida, we plan to go through Daytona Beach, so I can throw a flower on the water and say a prayer for Jim.

> Dear Mary Lou,
>
> I don't know your husband's name so will address this to you, and I do apologize for not answering sooner.
>
> Your letter touched me in many ways, but perhaps his death was the greatest crisis of my life. It was very hard to explain.
>
> Our love of flying was instilled in us from our relationship with Jimmy Doolittle, the famous aviator who led the raid on Japan in World War II. He lived in a duplex with us in Detroit. Influential and friendly best described him. We boxed with his sons. He died last week.

POSTSCRIPT ON JIM

Jim was my opposite. He took more risks though he wrote I was more at risk with my motorcycle. I'm still intrigued with flying and occasionally hang-glide.

I have three children. A daughter, a graduate of Roanoke, who administers a family trust. My oldest boy is a graduate of Tufts in accounting and public health and two years of business management from George Washington. The second son is a local builder, a graduate of American University.

Jim's body was never found. I talked with his Wing who followed his plane down and thought an explosion prevented his ejecting. His helmet was all that was recovered. I talked with the parents of Kolwaski, whose plane cut off the tail of Jim's plane after Jim signaled for a turn. Fellow pilots told me they flew combat-weary planes brought back from the South Pacific, that no sun gear had been issued, and that Kolwaski had been blinded by the sun.

I may have given you this information at our Arlington meeting (in summer of 1945) but I was still a little tight then.

I have Jim's name on my parents' gravestone in Arlington. There is a monument in Clarendon with his name as a World War II veteran who died in the service of his country.

Hope this will be of solace to you. It has been a help to me to share these thoughts with you. I wish the best to you and your family.

Sincerely,
David Peete

Madge and Mary Lou, Syracuse, 1945

Chapter Nine

The Summer of '45

I FINISHED MY JUNIOR YEAR and went home to Washington for the summer. I felt frozen inside, but fortunately Jane was coming, and we both got our jobs back with the British Army Staff. VE Day was just a little over a month after Jim's death, but the war was still in full swing in the Pacific against the "Nips," as Americans called them with great disaffection. Roosevelt had died the day after Jim, shocking the nation. We all thought he was immortal. Harry Truman had become president and was soon to have his finest—or worst—hour, dropping the atomic bomb on Hiroshima. Jane was now engaged to her West Point cadet and was to be married in August. We followed our routine of staying in town on Thursday night for our vegetarian dinner, and this time we really shopped—for her trousseau.

No one talked about Jim with me. Mother and Dad apparently felt that the best way to help me was to never mention his name. One night, shortly after I got home, I was sitting in the living room reading some of his letters and laughing at something he said. Mother was shocked. I think she thought I was cracking up.

When I returned to school for my senior year that fall, she burned his letters. I never forgave her for that. They were a chronicle of part of my life. Then, after I was engaged to your father, she threw away his pictures except for the small ones I had in my wallet. She had somehow missed a course on grief counseling. I met Jim's mother once for lunch, but she was already showing the signs of the breakdown she had later that summer that put her in a psychiatric hospital. We had not known each other well anyway, so we really could not share our grief. His brother David came home on leave to help look after his mother and took me out to dinner. I couldn't talk to him either; he was quiet and withdrawn.

Jane's marriage plans were accelerated when her future husband Salty was assigned to go overseas to Japan in the army of occupation. She was on the train on her way to Fort Sill, Oklahoma, to marry him when VJ Day was formally announced.

On August 14th, the war was over. The whole country celebrated with huge screaming crowds. My father would not let me out of the apartment. I had to listen to the bedlam on the radio. I was furious. Meanwhile, your father, that man who was still an unknown to me, happily celebrated in Louisville where he was in the Navy V-12 program studying to be an engineer. This did not mean everyone was now out of service. It took months, even years, for everyone to be mustered out. And of course, some were to remain in the reserves awaiting the next call to duty.

I was alone again. Dad decided to take matters into his own hands. He was tired of seeing his twenty-year-old daughter moping around like a young widow. Without consulting me, he invited a young major from his office, Tommy Moncure, for dinner. Tommy was from an old Southern family living in Alexandria, Virginia. He was blonde and had a baby face, so he seemed harmless enough. When he called and asked me for a date the next day, I accepted, mostly to please my father but also to get out of the house. On our first date, we drove to Annapolis for the day. I had never seen the Naval Academy, so I enjoyed it. He took numerous pictures of me sitting on cannons, which are in my photograph album from that era. I started going out with him a couple of times a week, but I could not bear the thought of his even holding my hand, much less kissing me goodnight. There certainly wasn't much in it for him, but he persevered. Toward the end of August, he picked me up one night and asked if it was all right if we went to a party his cousin Neville was having at the Marine bachelor officers' quarters. That was fine with me, as I did not like to be alone with Tommy. He told me Neville had just gotten back from Europe and was assigned to the Judge Advocate's office, the legal wing of the service.

Tommy Moncure and Mary Lou

I am sure there are scenes from your past life that you can see in your memory like a still photograph. The night I met Neville was one of those vignettes in my life, as he was to play a very important role in bringing me back to a reasonably normal emotional state. The Marine BOQ was a group of charming old buildings with little individual apartments for the unmarried marine officers. When Tommy and I walked in, I saw a very attractive dark young man in the uniform of a captain with the usual batch of ribbons across his chest—which I could never interpret although I certainly had a massive exposure to them. He was only a few inches taller than my 5'-6". His mother was a Moncure, and though his last name was Hall, he had inherited the French Moncure blood in his appearance, unlike his blonde cousin Tommy. He was twenty-six, six years older than I.

Mary Lou at Annapolis

After we were introduced, he took me back to his little kitchen to make me a drink. I asked for some sweet concoction like rum and coke, and he promptly told me that I should not drink garbage like that; it would make me sick. He made me a scotch and soda and told me I would learn to like it. I eventually did. I don't remember if he had a date that night, but we spent most of the evening talking to each other. He had finished two years of law school before his old college ROTC status had caused him to go into service about the same time as Dad had been called up. He had chosen the Marines. He liked politics and history and treated me like a person, not a featherbrained female. He was the first man I had met since Jim's death who aroused a tiny bit of interest in me. The next day, like a loyal cousin, he called and asked me for a date. My father was horrified when I accepted after he found out he was related to Tommy—a first cousin, no less. He thought he must be a rat to move in like that on his cousin's girlfriend, which I was not.

I could talk to Neville. He was the first person I really talked to about Jim. I told him that I did not think I could ever love another man or even stand to have one touch me. That was like throwing a gauntlet down to a Marine. By the time I started going out with Neville, it was only a few weeks before I had to go back to school. Syracuse was on the three-semester plan like most of the colleges during the war, so it started in late September. We did the usual things—went out to dinner, went to the hotel nightclubs and danced; and once, when I did not want to go home when everything closed, we joined an after-hours club. This was a gimmick to get around Washington's 2:00 AM curfew. The one we joined was on Massachusetts Avenue in the embassy area and was full of young embassy staffers, as well as the military. You brought your own bottle—scotch, of course—and bought set-ups at some exorbitant rate. We were not there for the drinks but rather for the conversation, the canned music, and the noise. Youth loves noise.

One day he called to ask me if I would like to go rollerskating. I had not skated since I was in high school. It sounded like fun. The indoor rink was down by the Potomac River in what must be the present Watergate area. Rock Creek Park snakes through the city and eventually winds up close to that area at one end. We rented our skates and joined all the kids on the floor. Everyone in the military had to wear their uniforms all the time. As a captain, Neville looked a bit out of place with all the young enlisted men and teenagers. We were having a great old time, eating popcorn and hot dogs and whirling around the floor.

All of a sudden, some young boys ran into us, and I fell. When Neville helped me up, I started to shake, shake so hard that my teeth were chattering. He knew battle fatigue when he saw it, so he hustled me off the floor, took off my skates, and put me in his car. By then, I was crying hysterically, the first time I had cried since the few weeks after Jim died. He drove into the park until he found a place to stop. He gave me his handkerchief—khaki-colored, of course—and comforted me like a father would a child. "Cry, Sweetheart, cry. It will do you good." By the time I stopped crying, Neville was kissing me, and the ice had finally started to melt around my heart. This was the barest beginning of a relationship between us. Shortly after that, I went back to school for my senior year. Neville and I did not write, but I knew he would be there when I came home for Christmas.

Much to my surprise, a few days before I was to leave for school, my old beau Brad turned up on my doorstep with a buddy of his from Yale. I had not seen Brad or heard from him in more than three years. In that time, he had graduated from high school, graduated from pre-med at Yale, and was starting his first year at Yale Medical School. He was in the Navy V-12 program, which was geared to train the necessary engineers and doctors that we had to have because of and in spite of the war. These young men were all accelerated through school with few leaves or breaks, unlike Jim who had been in the V-5 program. I suspect the Navy was more generous with their young airmen due to their hazardous profession. Also, the V-12 men took the standard curriculum of the various universities they attended. All were supposed to finish with their degrees plus a commission in the Navy, owing the Navy a certain amount of time for their education and becoming permanent reserve officers ready for any future war. Many were to serve in the Korean War.

We did not exactly start up where we had left off in the summer of '42. Lots of water had gone over the dam since then. I gave the two young men my standard two dollar tour of Washington, since neither had ever been there before. Mother had them to dinner, as she did with numerous service men who passed through Washington during that period. Before he left, Brad asked me if he could come to see me at Syracuse when he could get time off, and I agreed.

♥

Margarete and Lewis with Mary Lou at her Syracuse graduation

Chapter Ten

Graduation

I WENT BACK TO SYRACUSE for my senior year in late September. I was rushing chairman for Tri Delt, which involved directing the formal system of selecting the pledges who would be future sisters in Delta Delta Delta. We had a series of parties for four weekends along with the other sororities on campus, gradually getting down to the twenty young women we would invite to join—a barbaric system for those who are left out! After each party, we gathered in our chapter room, pruning our list, with many tears over those we were eliminating from consideration. I was happy when it was all over and we could settle down to school once more. My sorority was my home away from home during very bleak years, with close friendships and a warm and gracious mansion to live in; but the Greek system was then—and, I suspect, is now—a cruel way of destroying the self-esteem of young people who are not included. At that time, we had "quotas," which have since been outlawed by national Panhellenic rules. We could only take in twenty per cent Catholic girls in our pledge class. It is hard to see what threat they were supposed to offer. And, of course, we did not take in any Jews, Blacks, or, as far as I know, Asians or other races or ethnic groups. We were a very "Waspy" bunch of girls. One of our sophomore girls left Tri Delt when a friend of hers who was black could not be considered for membership. I lacked her courage. I was still too insecure though I could see the injustice of it.

The Winter Carnival

There were few men on campus that year of 1945-46. The war was over so late in the summer that most of them did not have time to matriculate. The GI College Bill was passed by Congress, and by the fall of 1946, the colleges and universities were overflowing with returning ex-GIs, including your father. But I seemed to have been fated to go through my four years of college in a very abnormal time—in fact, I timed it perfectly. There were no big football weekends, glamorous proms, or anything resembling the movies I had so avidly watched as a teenager in high school.

We did have Winter Carnival again that year, however. We built snow sculptures and had a Snow Ball. I asked my old pal Bill Pollard, who was by then in his first year at Long Island Medical College, to come for the weekend. Gloria's fiancé, Dick Lagergren, was coming for the weekend also. Gloria and I found a dressmaker, bought material, and each had a dress made, my first formal since I had been in college. Bill had a friend, Ed Pinckney, better known as Pinky, who was in Syracuse Medical School. He was married to a nice girl named Cathy, and they had a little one-bedroom apartment near campus. Dick, Gloria, Bill, and I spent quite a bit of the weekend at their apartment; and we became friends.

Not too long after that, Brad called me and said he would like to come for the next weekend. Cathy and Pinky asked us to come to dinner on Saturday night while Brad was there. The two boys enjoyed comparing notes on their curriculum and their anatomy bodies and dissection techniques—which, I suspect, was meant to impress or shock me.

I have no trouble explaining my relationship to Jim or Neville to you or myself. Brad is different. As your father describes him, he was a bit of a rascal, and, for some reason, women are attracted to rascals. There was definitely chemistry between us, but it was never love. He was a rather cold person, especially when the lights were on! That night at the Pinckneys', after we had eaten dinner and talked for a while, Pinky and Cathy retreated to their bedroom and told us to turn off the lights and lock the door when we left. Brad turned the lights off right away, and we reviewed our old techniques from the summer of '42. I think I was looking for someone to take Jim's place in my life, and I suspect I thought Brad might be the one, since I had known him even before I knew Jim. I was a mixed-up kid and had bad taste in men—at least, as far as he was concerned and if I was looking for a stable alliance.

He went back to Yale and, before leaving, asked me to come for a weekend at Yale later in the spring. My brother and sister-in-law were at Yale by then, Lewis working on his Ph.D. in physics on the GI Bill. Thus, it was easy to convince Mother and Dad that it would be nice for me to go to New Haven for a weekend to see them, seeing my old beau Brad on the side. As usual, I went off on the train to New York and then took the infamous New Haven Railroad to Yale. My father was out of the service by then and considerably more prosperous, so he sent me money to take Lewis, Margie, and Brad out to dinner one night.

Brad took me on a tour of the campus. I did not know I would eventually be living there with another man, my future and still unknown husband. I had to see the anatomy lab and his body, which I found to be surprisingly impersonal and dignified. The last stop on Saturday night was to see his room in the medical school dorm. He had conveniently gotten rid of his roommate. We looked at his textbooks and then sat down on his couch. After a few minutes, he picked me up and carried me to his bed—shades of Rhett Butler and Scarlett O'Hara! He was the first and only man who ever carried me to a bed. It was rather exciting, but my brain kicked into gear and I thought, "What on earth am I doing here?" I got up very hastily and said the famous old lines, "Take me home." He was a bit put out at me, but we had too many family ties for him not to do what I said. The next morning he took me to the train, and we parted a bit coolly. That was that for Brad, I thought. Fortunately, that was not that. We had one final, very important episode still to come.

I was in my last spring at Syracuse. I worked hard. My favorite professor was a Dr. Hepner, who wrote books and consulted on industrial psychology. I did not know how useful what I learned from him would be in my future life, starting at Yale with my future husband. We all started to make plans for our careers—though, as I have said before, women were not directed toward careers at that time apart from teaching and nursing. I know my parents assumed I would play around at working briefly and then get married and have children. They felt that my education was mostly to make me a good wife and mother and not to help me support myself. Little did they know that it would be used for a little of both and that I would work most of my adult life.

My friend Marilyn Johnson, better known as Jonnie, and I decided we would like to work and live in New York. Gloria was going to stay around Nutley, New Jersey, her home, as she was engaged and saving money to help furnish her future home. She had applied for a job as a decorator for a department store in Newark. Interior design had been her major in the School of Fine Arts. But first came graduation.

GRADUATION

Graduation was April 28th, 1946. I was twenty-one years old. Mother and Dad came to witness this great event. We wore black silk caps and gowns with our tassles on the correct side, to be flipped to the other side after we received our degree. Which side? I can't remember. Unfortunately, instead of graduating in the football stadium in the bright sunshine, we had a blizzard, and it had to be moved indoors to the field house, which was not very big or well ventilated. We had to wear our winter coats under our gowns to allow us to stand in line outdoors for an hour or so before we marched in. There were seven hundred in our graduating class, give or take a few. In spite of my rather frantic love life, I graduated Magna Cum Laude, seventh in my class. My little bookworm tendency survived my college years.

Then came the farewells and tears. We all swore we would visit each other frequently and write often, but the only two college friends I have kept up with are Gloria and Jonnie. Your father and I went back for my twentieth reunion, and I had a hard time remembering who most people were.

After graduation, Jonnie and I went to New York to try to find jobs and an apartment. We stayed with her sister in New Jersey and commuted into the city to walk the streets. Her major had been Latin American Studies and Languages, so she promptly found a job in the export division of a large bank. Then, hallelujah, I got a job in the personnel department of Macy's Department Store. I was thrilled. Next came the big letdown. Rent control, which had been in place all during the war, was now off. Moreover, thousands of people were out of the military and were looking for places to live. What we found, we could not afford. We finally gave up, supposedly temporarily, and Jonnie accepted her job and arranged to live with her sister. She was going to keep on looking for a small apartment for us, at which time I would return to the big city and find another job. I returned home depressed and disillusioned with the great big world out there that I was supposedly equipped to conquer. Mother and Dad were sympathetic but, I suspect, relieved. They did not want me to leave the nest and go off to live in a place like New York. After secret consultation, they came up with a plan. I had worked every summer while I was in college, had slaved away at school, so I was probably exhausted and could use a nice vacation. Why didn't I take the summer off and enjoy Washington?

I must digress a bit to tell you about my mother's situation. My Grandmother Lewis, Mama E, was mentally disturbed. I am sure it was Alzheimer's, but we had not heard of that disease then. With his daughters' help, my grandfather had hired a housekeeper and later a practical nurse to look after her. This required much commuting on my mother's part, as she was the only daughter not tied down with young children. Later that summer, it became necessary to put my grandmother in a nursing home where the quiet little lady who did not even say "darn" became very difficult to handle and swore like a trooper.

This left my grandfather, Papa E, who had been waited on hand and foot by his wife and daughters, in the company of the housekeeper, who was just a little older than my mother. Kim was very nice lady, a widow with one grown daughter. As the summer wore on, my grandfather, the pillar of dignified Fayetteville society, confided in his daughters that he thought he would divorce my grandmother and marry Kim. This bombshell resulted in gigantic phone bills as the daughters conferred on this scandalous situation. Naturally, Mother was elected to go to Fayetteville and reason with Papa.

So you see, my parents had additional reason to keep me under their wing. I was really needed at home to keep house for my father while Mother paid extended visits to Fayetteville to deal with her errant father.

♥

Chapter Eleven

A Belle of Washington

WHEN I FINALLY DECIDED to take my parents up on the invitation to take the summer off, I became quite enthusiastic about the idea. That is when I entered what I will call my Belle of Washington phase. It was not hard to be a Belle of Washington. The city was full of hundreds of eligible, charming young men either still in service, in the process of getting out, or already out and going back to school or jobs. Those who had finished their educations before the war were looking for a wife after wasting three or four years of normal courtship time.

Like most healthy young women, I was reasonably pretty in the Twiggy mode. I had long, slender legs, a twenty-one inch waist, and, at one hundred and ten pounds, I at last had some semblance of curves. I had long reddish-brown hair and, as they say about horses, good teeth. Since I had quit biting my fingernails at the age of thirteen, I devoted a great deal of time to my long, bright red nails that matched the bright red lipstick that all stylish young women wore. I also was educated, or so my diploma said. After Jim, I was not ready for another serious relationship. As a late bloomer, I just wanted male companionship—lots of male companionship. Thus, I did not turn out to be much of a housekeeper for my father. I didn't know how to cook anyway, and he sent his shirts to the laundry. If you recall, ironing was my only domestic skill. Instead, my father usually cooked dinner for me and then greeted my date of the evening at the door and talked to him while I finished getting ready. You were never supposed to be ready on time. Your date would think you were too eager.

The bulwarks of my male companionship were the three men whom my father referred to as "Mary Lou's Armed Forces." The first one and the favorite was my Marine captain. He was now out of uniform and back in Charlottesville at the University of Virginia, boning up on what he had studied before the war so he could start his senior year in law school there in the fall. Neville was the only one I kissed. I saved Saturday night for him, as he usually just came home on weekends. The second one was faithful Tommy, Neville's cousin, who was still in uniform as a major in the Army. I really felt awkward going out with him since I liked Neville, but my father had introduced him to me, and I felt an obligation when he asked me and I wasn't busy. The third was a new player.

Bill Cox was a commander in the Navy. I had met him at Christmas through an old family friend, Elliot Frank. Elliot had been a bank examiner with my father many years earlier, starting when he was only seventeen years old. As he grew up, he went into a bank in Chicago and became very successful. However, along the way, he had neglected to get married and thus had a girl in every port. He eventually married at the age of seventy. His Washington lady was Letitia Cox, Bill's older sister. Elliot had come for dinner during the Christmas season of 1945, and after dinner, he asked me to go with him to call on Letitia. When we got there, her baby brother Bill was there in all his glory—all 6' 4" and two hundred and seventy-five pounds of solid Navy muscle. He looked like Arnold Schwarzenegger, but a very shy version of Arnie. He had graduated from the Naval Academy before the war and had been at sea for at least five years, the more recent years as commander of a destroyer. You could really picture Bill standing on the poop deck, or whatever you call it, of a destroyer, peering through his binoculars and blasting submarines out of the water. But somehow, during all of that, this impressive man had not had time to develop the skills of talking to a woman. I suspect Elliot and Letitia planned our meeting, as it was obvious that at the age of thirty-two, Bill had to find a wife. He was a career Navy man but was to have a few years of shore duty—and this was the time to do it. His older brother, Ed, had no such problems, as he had been on cushy shore duty in the Army where he had very frequent contacts with ladies. More about that later. Their family was "Old Washington." General Cox, their father, was Commanding General of the Military District of Washington—a very prestigious post, more political than warlike. Bill, Elliot, Letitia, and I went out for a drink, and shy Bill talked to me. The next day he called and asked me for a date for the following Thursday night. I became his Thursday date for a while, and then I was flattered when he moved me up to Friday. I turned down Saturday, because I saved that for Neville. I have no idea what we talked about, but apparently we did talk, as I continued to go out with him about once a week until I was engaged to your father.

I must tell you about a party that Bill took me to early on in my Friday night slot in his wife search. He had been invited, with his date, to a party in a country home in Virginia, which adjoined Washington and was part of the suburban area. The time was eight o'clock. Mother, as usual, was out of town coping with her helpless father. Dad decided I was starting to travel in rather fast company, a bit beyond my capability to handle at the age of twenty-one. He assured me that no doubt these people would be drinking, and he insinuated that I had to be very careful not to overindulge and either disgrace myself by collapsing at the party or, worse, be seduced by shy Bill on the way home. Neville had already taught me to sip on a scotch and soda, so I never collapsed anywhere. In spite of my protestations, Dad insisted that the best protection against alcoholic beverages was to have a good meal under your belt. Thus, he cooked me a sirloin steak dinner, complete with a salad and baked potato. And, like Mammy did to Scarlet before she went to the barbeque, he stood over me while I ate every bite.

   I put on my best little silk dress, homemade by the dressmaker in Syracuse, and went off with Bill in all of his Navy finery, complete with rows of ribbons across his chest. The party was in honor of Lady Iris Mountbatten, cousin of then Princess Elizabeth, whom Bill's social climbing brother was dating. When we arrived at the country home, we found a beautiful estate complete with butler. Bill did not have a snobbish bone in his body but was a very eligible Washington bachelor. He hovered over me like a mother hen, so I would not be uncomfortable in this rather well-heeled and older company. I soon found out that there were just twelve of us in the "drawing room," where cocktails were being served by the butler. I was very disappointed in Lady Iris, a rather horsey looking woman in her mid-thirties rather than the fairy tale English beauty that I had imagined an aristocrat to be. Then came the unexpected blow. Dinner was announced. Dinner??? We sat down in the elegant dining room and were served the soup course by the butler and his helper. Footman??? I managed to swallow the soup, which was then followed by the shrimp cocktail, salad, the fish course, the entrée, and the dessert—all, of course, served with the proper wine. I handled the silverware OK, as I knew you worked from the outside in, but the food was another story. I picked a little at each course, enough so I hoped the hostess would not be offended. She probably did not notice anyway, as I cannot recall any of the "ladies" addressing another word to me, other than the hostess saying "How d'ya do?" when Bill introduced me. Then, believe it or not, the ladies adjourned to the drawing room while the men had brandy and cigars.

   Bill gave me a sympathetic look when I left with the five barracudas, who continued to ignore me in the so-called drawing room. The evening mercifully came to a close. Driving back to Washington, I thought it best to confess to Bill that I had eaten a huge dinner before going, explaining some of my father's reasoning. He laughed so hard he had to stop the car, and then he assured me that he was not the slightest bit impressed with the pseudo-Virginia aristocracy, and he would not inflict it on me or himself again. Meanwhile, back in the drawing room, I am sure they were all saying, "Where on earth do you suppose he got her?" Another time Bill took me to a cocktail party at the Chilean embassy. That was very exciting. Dad had learned his lesson and did not make me eat before I went that time.

In addition to these three men, my pal Bill Pollard was home for the summer between his freshman and sophomore year in medical school, so we did things together. He remained a friend for many years through notes at Christmas and was the one who addressed our wedding invitations in his fine script. His bride later wore my wedding dress—which she failed to return for three years. The fragile material was ruined by perspiration by the time I got it back. Bill did not have a particularly happy marriage with her. When she died of kidney failure at a fairly young age, he happily married a very nice widow. The last we heard, they were living in Charlottesville, Virginia, where he was a family practitioner.

Bill Pollard and Mary Lou

I had an assortment of other casual beaus, including a medical student from Syracuse, who lived in a nearby Maryland town and was in Washington occasionally. Then there was Jimmy Trimble, the son of the congressman from Arkansas who had been Dad's best friend in college. Jimmy was finishing up at West Point and invited me there for a weekend, but it sounded rather dull to me, so I never did go. West Point was more like a convent than Allegheny had been! I dated a law student from Georgetown University, whom I had met on the mall in front of the Washington Monument when one of my girlfriends was visiting. I had to be pretty cagey with Mother and Dad as to exactly how I had met him, as they never would have approved of my going out with anyone without a proper introduction. He was a Kennedy-type Irish Catholic from Boston, John Quigley, so our relationship never would have gone anywhere, even if we had wanted it to. Catholics and Protestants married only with extreme difficulty and family disapproval on both sides in those days.

In the midst of my busy social life in mid-July, Brad called and told me that he was going to be in Lake Bluff in early August on vacation and why didn't I come out at the same time and visit Betty and Harmon, my aunt and uncle. That sounded like a good idea for two reasons. The first was that I had to check the rascal out once more. The second was that I was to be in Gloria's wedding in late August and she had sent me material to make my dress. All of Mother's sisters sewed. Mother did not! Once when I was about nine years old, she and her best friend Dorothy decided to make a dress for me. Dorothy's daughter was older, and she rejected the plan to make one for her also. I remembered that dress very well and felt that Mother and I could not tackle my bridesmaid's dress. On the other hand, Betty was a wonderful seamstress. She had a new baby, my cousin David, whom I had not seen. So after consultation with Betty, who really wanted me to come, it was decided that I would go out for two weeks. I did not mention Brad. That would not have been psychologically sound. I also did not mention to Neville that I was going to see another man. That would not have been prudent either. So off I went on the train to Chicago. I should have gotten a Frequent Railroad Bonus, as they give them to frequent flyers.

After a mandatory evening with Betty and Harmon, the next night I went out with Brad. We went to one of the little roadhouses, as they called the highway bars, and spent most of the evening pleasantly reminiscing about our summer of '42. This was the first time both of us had been back there together. He was interested in hearing about Jane, who was in Japan with her husband. We talked about getting out his sailing canoe while we were there. All went well until we started home. We drove down to the beach in Lake Forest, which was the local Lover's Lane spot at night. No one was there. We got out of the car and walked down the beach in our bare feet, hand in hand. Then we went through sort of a repeat of what had happened in his dorm room at Yale. I said, "Take me home," and he was very angry. Obviously, we still had different agendas.

That would have been the end of our relationship except . . .

John Walbridge, Jr.

Chapter Twelve

John Walbridge Arrives

BRAD HAD MADE ARRANGEMENTS for us to go out on a double date the next night with his old fishing buddy, John Walbridge, who had gotten out of the Navy rather belatedly because he had chosen to go out in the Fleet as a seaman second-class at the end of the war rather than accepting an ensign's commission and staying in the reserves after finishing his Navy V-12 training in engineering. I was to find this out the next evening in animated conversation on his dislike of military life—and particularly Naval officers. But I am getting ahead of my story.

The next evening, Brad, John Walbridge, Nan Shields—a high school friend of the two boys who was John's date—and I went out together. We went to one of the usual local spots for beer, conversation, and dancing to the juke box. John, Nan, and I had a good time while Brad glowered quietly. At the end of the evening, Brad took Nan home first, which was the custom, since he was driving. Then he took me home, which was not the custom but was fine with me. Sulky or not, young men were gentlemen then, with manners drilled into them by their parents. Brad started to get out of the car to open my door and take me to the house. I jumped out and said "I can get in by myself!" "Bang!" went the door. That was the last time I ever saw Brad.

John Walbridge in the Navy

Bright and early next morning John Walbridge called and asked me to go out that night. Here was another rat like Neville—only instead of asking his cousin's girlfriend out, he was asking one of his best friends' girlfriends. Women are vindictive! I said yes, mostly to get even with Brad. I have no idea where we went or what we did on our first date. It was not love at first sight, and no matter how I quiz your father, he does not remember what possessed him to jeopardize his friendship with Brad. Maybe with men, they just think all is fair in love and war. Anyway, we hit it off on that first date enough for us to start going out every night together. Meanwhile, my patient aunt and uncle wondered about the fickleness of young women. During the days of this preliminary courtship period, Brad and John played golf together during the day. I could never wheedle out of John what they talked about, and now he

JOHN WALBRIDGE ARRIVES

has long since forgotten, not being blessed with my memory for trivia.

John happily joined beach parties with my aunt and uncle, and they liked him. Somewhere in this period came our first kiss, which I am sure was not long after we started dating, as your father is not a patient man. I did not meet his parents, as we were not yet that committed to each other. I liked him. He had unusually nice manners and was kind like Neville. He was sexy and macho like Brad. He was intelligent, like all my boyfriends had been. He was good looking and sweet like Jim. During that period, he was accepted at Yale for his junior year after his two years at the University of Louisville in V-12. I helped him celebrate.

There was one small problem to spoil our budding romance. It was Gloria's wedding and that stupid dress that I supposedly had gone out to Chicago to make with Betty's help. She was getting very nervous about it. I hated the dress material. It was a purplish fuchsia rayon faille, a color that was lovely around Gloria with her fair complexion and awful on me with my sallow skin. However, I had no choice. Betty finally told John that we could not meet again until the dress was finished. She had a baby to take care of during the daytime plus two other children, so we had to sew at night. We finally finished it just in time for me to leave to go back to Washington and then take the train to Newark for the wedding. John and I bid each other fond farewell after he asked me if he could come to see me in Washington on his way to Yale. He had never been there and was eager for my "two dollar tour."

Gloria's wedding was beautiful, complete with a bagpiper in honor of her half-Scots heritage. In spite of my purplish dress, I looked reasonably respectable with the help of a little blusher. I saw many of my Tri Delt sisters who had come for the wedding, most of whom I never saw again. Then it was back to Washington to take up where I had left off with Neville and my Washington beaus. I was not ready to burn any bridges yet.

John arrived in early September and had to sleep on a bed in my father's bedroom while Mother and I shared my twin beds. He drove his mother's red Ford, which he had bought from her.

He called it "The Red Cadillac," and I did not know the difference. In fact, I thought it was a Cadillac long after we were married. Since I did not drive, I did not know one car from another. Our romance took a few more steps forward during that visit, but we were not ready to commit ourselves only to each other. I was having too much fun in Washington, and he had unfinished business with his girlfriend Jane, whom he had known in Louisville. Also, he was looking forward to his first year of real college without a Navy officer looking over his shoulder. Naturally, I had to tell him about my commander, whom he said he would punch in the nose if he ever met him. He really did dislike Navy officers, particularly my Navy officer.

After a few days of doing the Washington scene, he headed for New Haven. The day he left, my brother called me from New Haven to tell me that Brad had been killed in an automobile accident on the way from New Jersey to New Haven. He had been visiting an unmarried aunt he was very close to, and she was driving him back to school. It was a terrible shock. He was just twenty-one years old. I did not grieve for him. I finally knew that I was not ever in love with Brad. Mother and I cried for his parents and his little sister and for the brilliant young man who would never use his fine mind or live the life he should have lived. John called me from Yale when he heard. He was in shock too, and I think he wanted to know how I was. Now there were just John and Neville I cared about.

Neville was starting his senior year at the University of Virginia Law School. He invited me to come down for a weekend in September. His old undergraduate fraternity was having a party on Saturday night, and he wanted to show me Charlottesville, the university, and Monticello, Jefferson's home. By then, I think if I said I was going off to join a harem, Mother and Dad would just have sighed and wished me well. They had no idea who was winning in this rather spirited competition that seemed to be going on. So they said to go ahead. I think I must have taken a bus to Charlottesville. Neville had gotten me a room at the inn in the historic downtown area. The university was a very important part of the town and was one of the country's great old schools, along with the Ivy League colleges. It war perfectly respectable for me to stay in the hotel, as in those days no man would dare to go to the room of an unmarried woman. Hotel managements, particularly in the South, were quite stodgy about morals. On Saturday morning Neville took me to breakfast, and then we toured Monticello, which was very exciting for me. He was an admirer of Jefferson and was very knowledgeable about his life and the things in the house. They were just beginning to restore it, attempting to retrieve lost pieces of furniture, or at least similar pieces, so the house was rather sparsely furnished. I remember the dumbwaiter in one of the rooms, which Neville told me Jefferson had invented. I also remember his high, short bed, which required steps to get into. Of course, it was swathed in draperies "to keep out the drafts." I think we must have gone to a football game in the afternoon and then out to dinner. That night was the party at his fraternity house.

As I have done throughout this mini-novel, I must digress once more to describe the nomenclature of that time. All Southern men, particularly Virginians, called young women by pet names. Tommy and Bill Pollard called me "Honey." Neville called me "Honey," "Sweetheart," or "Darling," depending on the occasion. So did Jim, though he was not Southern. Bill, my commander, called me "Mary Lou," and I am sure that when he eventually married, he called his wife "Mrs. Cox" or some such formal name. He was the exception. Your father called me "Sweetheart" or "Baby," of all the inappropriate names for a tall, skinny girl. I rather missed this pet name custom when I eventually settled in the North.

Back to the party. The fraternity house was full of Virginians, who immediately greeted Neville and me with such prattle as "Hi, Sweetheart" to me and "Where have you been hiding her, you old rascal" to Neville. They were serving some kind of well-laced punch, which someone immediately brought to me. From then on, my glass was never allowed to be empty. Neville was doing a bit of a slow burn, but that would not stop aggressive Southern males, as they all were. The University of Virginia was an all-male college at that time, so there were considerably more men than women at the party, which just made the competition more heated. As I was rather forcibly made to abandon my usual sipping of one scotch and soda, I began to feel a bit giddy. The punch tasted innocent, but believe me, it was not. All at once, the room felt very warm, and it seemed to be moving slightly.

From the time I first met Neville, he had always been very protective. This was probably due to his being older and considerably more mature. When he saw my dilemma, he came to my rescue and asked if I would like a bit of fresh air, which I certainly needed. He was more than happy to remove me from the claws of the predators anyway. We drove off to the environs of Monticello, and he stopped the car and said, "Sweetheart, we are going to take a nice long walk," which we did. He very kindly did not remind me that he had taught me to sip on one scotch and soda. He was the one who had thrust me into that den of iniquity, so he really could not say much. By the time we got back to the car, I felt considerably better.

Neville had never asked for any commitment from me; I think he felt he could not push me with Jim still a ghostly presence. He knew I was going out with other men, but he must have realized that I was not serious about any of them, as I was pretty much available to him when he came home. He always seemed to be able to figure me out, which would have been an unnerving trait to have in a husband. I was very comfortable and half in love with him, but there was a little spark missing. Maybe he was too much like my father. He knew I had been in Chicago for two weeks, and I think he realized that there might be someone else threatening our relationship besides my gaggle of miscellaneous male friends in Washington. Also, we had never gone on double dates with anyone, so his fraternity party was the first place he had to watch me with other men, and he obviously did not like it. Thus, when we got back to the car, gentle Neville became a bit more aggressive. He figuratively seized me by the hair and said, "Look, woman, I am tired of putting up with your shenanigans.

We need to have some kind of understanding and get down to basics," which he proceeded to do. When I came up for air, I said something like, "Hey, Neville. What do you think you are doing?" At which point he recovered his inbred good manners and apologized. Then he told me he was in love with me and wanted to marry me when he finished school. He had not intended to ask me that way. He wanted me to meet his parents and to give me a ring, but the situation rather forced his hand. Once, the previous summer, we had driven out to Alexandria and gone past his parents' charming pre-Civil War home. He wanted me to go in and meet them, but I had begged off on the excuse that we would be popping in on them unannounced and that did not seem proper. He did not press it. Now I was caught off guard by his proposal. No one had ever said, "Will you marry me?" to me before.

Jim and I had drifted into the plan to marry. There was never a moment when he asked me. After all the movies I had gone to in high school, I should have had a nice Hollywood-type of response, but instead I felt like a tongue-tied teenager. I was both surprised and flattered, but I knew I could not say yes. If I had not met John Walbridge, I think I would have. We had a good, solid relationship, and I am sure Neville would have made a very good husband. He would have spoiled me like my parents did and would only have expected me to be a good wife and mother. I know he would never have let me work. That would have been a blow to his manhood. My children would have Southern drawls, and I would not be allowed to express my liberal damn-Yankee views too loudly. But it did not happen. There was that darn John Walbridge hovering in the background. I told Neville that I did not think I was ready to make that decision yet. He would have to give me more time. So the weekend ended on an indecisive note. We could not make plans to see each other again for a while, as he was catching up on his studies after a four-year hiatus, and I had things planned for early that fall.

After that end of the summer weekend, I decided I should look for a job. Washington was not loaded with job opportunities at that time, as so many people who had come there in the war effort wanted to stay. And I was not exactly well trained for a business office, not being able to type. Mother and Dad suggested I go to a business school and learn typing and shorthand, which would help with any job. However, first they dangled another plum in front of me. Mother had to go back to Fayetteville to deal with her father and mother again at the same time that Dad was invited to teach at and address the New York State Bankers' Association, which was holding its annual convention in Quebec City. That was to be in mid-October and was to last almost a week. Naturally, Dad was to be a guest with all expenses paid, so he proposed that I go with him instead of Mother. They would be delighted to pay for my extra room. We all know that bankers spend their depositors' money like water, and the New Yorkers were no different. I had never been out of the country, and to go to French Canada sounded fantastic to me. I said I would be happy to go. My father told me to buy some clothes, so I would be properly decked out for all the glamorous occasions. Clothes were once more available after the war years, so he did not have to ask me twice to go shopping. Mother and I took the charge cards and spent a couple of days touring the Washington department stores—Hecht's, Woodward Lothrop, and Garfinckle's. This was long before anyone had ever heard of a "mall." I bought a beautiful grey pinstripe suit, which would still be in style today, since skirts were still wartime short, as mandated by the Federal government to save fabric. I also got a matching felt cloche-type hat and high-heeled black pumps. We found a soft, swirly pink chiffon evening dress trimmed in black velvet ribbons and one or two "afternoon" dresses. These, interspersed with my rather limited wardrobe, made me feel I could cope with any banker.

Before taking off on this exciting trip, I went to New Haven in early October for a football weekend with my newest beau, John Walbridge. I very properly stayed with my brother and sister-in-law. Lewis was working on his Ph.D. in physics and was set to get his preliminary master's degree that coming spring. Due to the severe housing shortage caused by the returning vets, many of whom were married, the university bought a number of surplus

Mary Lou and John, 1946

army Quonset huts and put them down on the athletic practice field. With the help of a few partitions and a little plumbing, they became home to many of the married students. Luxurious they were not! For one thing, they were level with the ground, which was pure sand due to the foot traffic on the athletic field. This did not bother me, as I only occupied the couch in the tiny living room for a very limited amount of time that weekend anyway. John and I went to the football game and partied with his new cronies, whom I was to get to know much better the following year after we were married.

Yale College, the undergraduate portion of Yale University, had approximately four thousand students. They lived in what were called living colleges, each of which surrounded a central courtyard accessible through iron gates from the street. The living college a student was assigned to after his freshman year became his permanent affiliation within the university. John's was Branford College; John III's was Davenport College when he attended Yale twenty-odd years later. The buildings were divided into suites with a living room, two bedrooms, and usually a fireplace, which was not used very often since there were not many trees to chop down in the city of New Haven. Surrounding Branford was a moat four or five feet deep—fortunately not filled with water as in Old England. The sills of the first floor windows were probably nine feet above the floor of the moat.

Yale had strange rules, at least to a girl who had gone to considerably less relaxed colleges. At that time, the undergraduate college of Yale was all male. It eventually admitted women partway through John III's period of schooling there. But in 1946, women were allowed to go into the rooms in the dorms up until eight o'clock at night. After that, a campus policeman was stationed at the gate and would allow no female to pass through. If you were already there, you could stay all night as far as they were concerned. There was just the problem of getting in. Unfortunately, on the Saturday I was there after the football game, we had gone out to dinner and gotten back to Branford for a party too late for me to run the gauntlet through the iron gate. What a dilemma! Here was this lovely party with all of his friends and their dates, and we could not get to it. However, your father is always creative in his thinking. We went around to one side of the building and threw pebbles at a window until some of the men heard and leaned out to ask what our problem was. John explained, and they were happy to cooperate in getting me in. We got down in the moat, John boosted me up on his shoulders, and the fellows pulled me into the party. Then all John had to do was to go around to the main gate and walk in. I was immediately embraced into the crowd and promptly forgot about John. I assumed he would get there eventually, going the long way around. It was a great party with lots of singing and revelry, so I did not miss him at first. After about forty-five minutes, I became a bit alarmed. I started thinking of faithful Neville, who would never abandon me at a party like that. Finally, an anxious John showed up. He had boosted me into the wrong party and had been searching the building for me. By the time I went home to get ready for my Canadian trip, I was thinking, "Is this love?" I would ponder that.

JOHN WALBRIDGE ARRIVES

The Canadian trip was wonderful. We took a special train from New York City with the New York bankers and their wives, I in my gorgeous pinstripe suit, pampered by all the elderly bankers. (I thought they were elderly anyway). We stayed in the Chateau Frontenac with my room overlooking the city of Quebec and the St. Lawrence River. I entertained with room service, serving hot chocolate and cookies that became famous among our little group there as a pleasant change from the free-flowing booze that was served everywhere else. My lady friends and I toured the fort, the churches, and a beautiful Carmelite convent where nuns dressed in white habits prayed perpetually in front of the altar. There we bought beautiful handmade handkerchiefs trimmed in exquisite lace and other linens. At the first dinner, they served salmon as the second course, which I thought was the entrée. I had eaten so much salmon during the war that I could hardly bear the sight of it. Then came an exquisite baron of beef, dripping rare juices, such as none of us had seen since before the war. In fact, I had never seen beef like that, since my mother tended to cremate meat.

The week finally came to an end, and we headed back home on the special train. On the way, I started to get a sore throat. By the time we finally arrived in Washington, I also had a fever along with other aches and pains. We did not have a doctor at the time. We had been under the care of the army and had gone to Walter Reed Army Hospital for our few ailments. My father knew I was sick when I stayed home in the evenings instead of pursuing my male companionship. We used all the old-time remedies like Vicks, aspirin, and gargling salt water. About a week after we got home, I woke up one morning with every gland in my body swollen grotesquely. I also had a raging fever and could not swallow. My father was finally really frightened when I could not get out of bed, and he began to search frantically for a doctor who would come over to the house. When the strange doctor arrived and looked me over, he informed my father that I either had acute leukemia or infectious mononucleosis, and I would have to come in and get a blood test to determine which one it was. Obviously, since I am still alive, it turned out to be the latter, the famous "kissing disease," which I jolly well deserved. I was very sick, and even with the help of the then new sulpha drugs, it was well into November before I started to feel a little bit better. I lost five of the precious pounds I had worked so hard to put on. It was at least a year before I completely recovered and managed to get them back. My illness postponed my proposed business school until the class that started after Christmas.

That was OK with me, as my sins were finally catching up with me. Bill, my commander, called and invited me to the Army-Navy game in Philadelphia, which was Thanksgiving weekend. He proposed that we would stay with Navy friends of his. He would have the wife call my mother and assure her that we would be properly chaperoned so she would have absolutely no worries about my reputation. That was not what I was worried about. I was afraid that one of these days Bill would do the same thing Neville had done and seize me by the hair, and I had no idea what I would say or do if he did this. I stammered about how I would have to let him know, as I did not think my parents would approve of a weekend like that—which, as you know, was a big laugh. Then Neville called and said he planned to take a break before exams and would like for me to go to the Army-Navy game with him. He did not say where we would stay. This became a terrible dilemma as Neville and Bill would both have tickets on the Navy side of the field, and if I went with one of them, I was sure to run into the other. I really wanted to see the game with all of its pageantry and excitement, and I figured this would be the last chance I would have unless I married Neville, which, by now, I pretty much knew I wasn't going to do. Or was I? I really wanted to go with Neville and, as I had with Brad, check him out once more. Then your father solved my problem.

He called and invited himself for Thanksgiving weekend. Having been very honest with him all along about Bill and Neville, I told him they had both invited me to this exciting game and I especially wanted to go. That is when he delivered his ultimatum, "Look, Baby, it is either them or me." How could I have let him push me around like that? But I said, "OK, I guess it is you." The fatal commitment! I told Neville I was having company for Thanksgiving and could not go. He did not pursue it. He told me he would see me at Christmas after he had finished his exams. I still have not seen an Army-Navy game. I almost saw half of one when Navy played Louisville at your father's fiftieth Navy V-12 reunion, but, at the last minute when it did not start until late afternoon after an all-day series of festivities, we faded away and took a nap instead. I guess I was still tired from staying up every night until 2:00 AM when I was young.

♥

Miss Mary Lou Sailor, John Walbridge, Jr. Announce Engagement

Mr. and Mrs. Vance L. Sailor of Washington, D. C., recently announced the engagement of their daughter, Mary Lou, to John Tuthill Walbridge, Jr. of Sunrise avenue, Lake Bluff. Mr. Walbridge is the son of the senior John T. Walbridges.

Miss Sailor is a niece of Mrs. Harmon H. Woodworth of Ravine Forest drive, and has visited frequently in Lake Bluff. She is a graduate of Syracuse university. Mr. Walbridge is in his junior year at Yale.

No immediate plans have been made for the wedding.

Chapter Thirteen

Engaged!

BACK TO THAT LONG AGO Thanksgiving weekend. When your father arrived, I made it obvious to him that he had goofed up my social affairs by intruding into my life over a period of only three months. He made it obvious to me that I had goofed up his life also, including his relationship with his Louisville girlfriend Jane and his very enjoyable bachelorhood at Yale. That weekend is when we negotiated our engagement. His idea was that we would become engaged at Christmas and then get married on some far-away date, like perhaps two or three years hence. Meanwhile, I would give up all of my male companionship and stay home with my mother and father, perhaps getting a job and going to business school. He was not too interested in the details of what I did, as long as I dumped all of my gentlemen friends. My idea was that I would keep my male friends indefinitely and at some far-away date like two or three years hence, we would become engaged and get married the next day. Something had to give.

We both knew deep down that we were right for each other, although it was not a convenient time for either of us to become engaged or get married. But we were each afraid we would lose the other if we did not make some kind of compromise and commitment. With great diplomacy, we hammered out our nuptial agreement, mostly parked in Rock Creek Park, my private love nest. He would give me a ring at Christmas time, I would notify my male companionship that I was no longer available, and we would get married in June after school was through for the summer. We would then join the myriad of student couples on the Yale campus for his senior year. I did not tell my parents of this plan. They did not know until they saw the ring. I received the ring before a party we went to in Virginia that a Yale friend of John's was having on New Year's Eve. It snowed that night, and we had to slip-slide home on the awful uncleared roads. They had no snowplows. It was an omen of my life-to-come in the frozen North.

But once more I am ahead of my story. There was still Neville, whom I had to notify. He was busy with exams and did not call me until he got home for Christmas vacation. I remember our conversation well, as I was very nervous about having to tell him. I should have written him, but I was too chicken. I had not gotten my ring yet, as John was only coming after Christmas on his way back to school, when he would spend New Year's Eve with me. Neville said, "Hello, Sweetheart. How are you?" I stammered a bit and asked him about his exams, and then I said, "Neville, I have something to tell you. I am engaged." (Of course, I did not have the ring yet. More about that later.) There was a stunned silence on the line. Then I said, "Can't we still be friends?" At that point Neville said, "Go to Hell!" and hung up.

I always seemed to have dramatic farewell scenes with my boyfriends. This one was like the others—only not ending in a tragedy as it had with Jim and Brad. I never saw Neville again. I assume he eventually settled down in Alexandria to practice law and married some lucky woman, who got a very nice husband. I had wasted a year and a half of his life, but he gave a great deal to me, and I will always be grateful.

There was no problem notifying Bill of my engagement. He was a Stoic, so I assume he just inserted someone else in my Friday slot. Several years later, Mother sent me the announcement from the Washington papers of his wedding to some Washington socialite. I am sure she fitted into the formal dinner party circuit better than I did on my first try.

Since I had notified my male companionship that I was no longer available at the beginning of the Christmas holidays, I was stranded at home with only the company of my parents. Meanwhile, John, unbeknownst to me, had my ring tucked into his pocket while he decided to kiss the girls goodbye. He went through Indianapolis, where his ex-girlfriend Jane now lived, to check her out once more. Obviously, we were two doubting Thomases and had to cover all the loose ends. He did not tell me he was going to see Jane. He knew better. In fact, he did not tell me for quite a while. His version of the story is that her finger was too fat for my ring, so he made it through without giving it to her. He slipped it on my finger New Year's Eve, 1946, just before the clock struck twelve. We had known each other for four months.

I should mention that I had a job between Thanksgiving and Christmas. It was temporary but fit in with my plans to go to business school after the holidays. It was selling perfume at Hecht's Department Store. The nice perfumes came in very large containers at that time, and you had to pour the perfume into small bottles measured in ounces. White Shoulders was new that year, and I still gag at the occasional sniff of it. The large bottles you poured from were very valuable, and I was extremely nervous about dropping one and owing the store all of my wages plus more. Fortunately, this did not happen. The windows of Hecht's were done in a Snow White and the Seven Dwarfs theme, so all day long I heard "Hi Ho, Hi Ho, it's off to work we go." When I hear that song, I am back behind the perfume counter selling White Shoulders.

♥

Mary Lou in her wedding dress

Chapter Fourteen

The Wedding

MOTHER AND DAD WERE a bit dubious about my hasty romance, but Betty Woodworth assured them that John came from quite a respectable family. Then, when my father found out that John played cribbage, he was accepted into the bosom of the family. My parents' marriage had started rather financially insecure, so they must have figured we would survive getting married with no income except the GI Bill. In fact, they probably thought it would do me good. During the holidays, we selected our wedding date—June 14, 1947.

When John went back to school, Mother and I started making plans. I did not want a big wedding, but Mother and Dad did. Mother had eloped, so she had always had a deep-seated frustration at never having walked down the aisle in virginal white. The first job was to reserve the church and the minister. Our wedding was to be in the chapel of Mount Vernon Place Methodist Church in Washington. The main sanctuary was too big, so we selected the chapel, which held about two hundred. Then we reserved the Carlton Hotel for the reception. The ceremony was to be at 8:00 in the evening with the reception afterwards. Washington was too hot in June to get married in the daytime without air conditioning, which churches did not have at that time. Then we had to buy a wedding dress, which then as now you had to order several months ahead. I believe it is usually a season ahead. My dress was a bit more ruffley than I wanted, but it was partly Mother's wedding, so I caved in. After all of this was done, I told John over the phone that my dress was ordered. I think it all came home to him at that moment what he had done. I suspect he did not quite believe that he was getting married on June 14th. That was not a real date! It was some time in the far-flung future, and here I was with a wedding dress. We commuted back and forth, I to New Haven and he to Washington, and he finally decided he was hopelessly ensnared by love and lust.

I had not met his family. I had gotten a gracious note from his mother and another from his sister, Ruth. They were anxious to meet me and invited me to come out during John's spring break. Mother and Dad thought this was a good idea and so it was decided, with me staying at Betty and Harmon's. Next came the problem of how to get there. John planned to drive, but it would not be proper for me to drive on a three-day trip with my fiancé without a chaperone. John, being very resourceful, rounded up a chaperone. He was a weird freshman named Jim Goff. He did not really want to waste three days of his vacation driving with us, but he had spent the money his family had sent him to take the train home, so he had no choice. To save time and distance, I took the train to New Haven. After I stayed all night with Lewis and Margie, the three of us embarked in the Red Cadillac for Lake Bluff on a clear, sunny early spring day.

The first day we got to know Jim better than we really cared to. His mother and stepfather were neighbors of John's family and were also good friends of my aunt and uncle. His stepfather was chief justice of the Illinois Supreme Court, and his mother was a charming Southern belle from Virginia who had lost her first husband in a hunting accident. He had fallen off a horse and broken his neck. Jim and his younger brother were sent off to live with their wealthy grandmother when his mother, Margo, fell apart after her husband's sudden death. They lived with their grandmother for seven years until she died. Jim told us he had murdered her with Sani Flush, and we have never been quite sure whether or not he was telling the truth. Jim eventually became a lawyer, a profession he was well suited for.

Listening to these fascinating tales, we headed across New York State down into Pennsylvania—the southern route. As the afternoon wore on, it started to snow. The snow got heavier and thicker until we could barely see the road. Highways were not interstates. This was a state highway going through farm country between small towns. Finally, the Red Cadillac gave up and stalled in a deep drift that had been whipped up by the blizzard winds. I had no boots and was wearing heels and my spring coat. It was a rather serious situation. It was starting to get dark.

We could see a farmhouse off in the distance up a long driveway. Jim said he would go to the farmhouse and try to get someone to come and pull us out of the drift. He disappeared up the road, while John and I huddled together to keep from freezing to death. An hour went by. We were becoming very concerned about Jim. Had he fallen into a drift and frozen to death? About that time he appeared, looking quite chipper. The farmer had invited him to sit down to dinner with them after calling a snowplow to come and rescue us. Naturally, he accepted. He claimed they had had squirrel stew. We were all starved by that time, and he thought there was no sense in all three of us starving and freezing to death. The snowplow arrived before it became pitch dark, and we followed it into a little Pennsylvania town to a small fleabag hotel. We were so cold, hungry, and exhausted that we would have slept in the farmer's barn. The boys had a room together, and I had a tiny room with something that looked like an army cot for a bed. I pulled back the blanket and saw little beetles scurrying around on the bed. Needless to say, I did not sleep well.

It took us two more days to reach Lake Bluff, with Jim complaining bitterly from the backseat. I do not remember where our other stops were, but I must have been able to take a bath someplace before I had to meet my future in-laws. John's family was very friendly and welcoming to me. I immediately fell in love with his father, who had the laidback sense of humor his son had inherited. My mother-in-law to be was a bit more reserved. She did comment that she always thought John would marry someone small and blond—but not in an unkind way.

Vance Sailor and Mary Lou

THE WEDDING

When it came time to return to New Haven, Jim backed out of his job as chaperone. No way was he going to go through that again, he told us. John's mother sighed and said that if my mother did not object to my driving back without a chaperone, there was not too much she could say about it. My mother did not have a great deal of choice. John's dad laughed and winked at me. The trip was uneventful. Winter had breathed its last on the trip there.

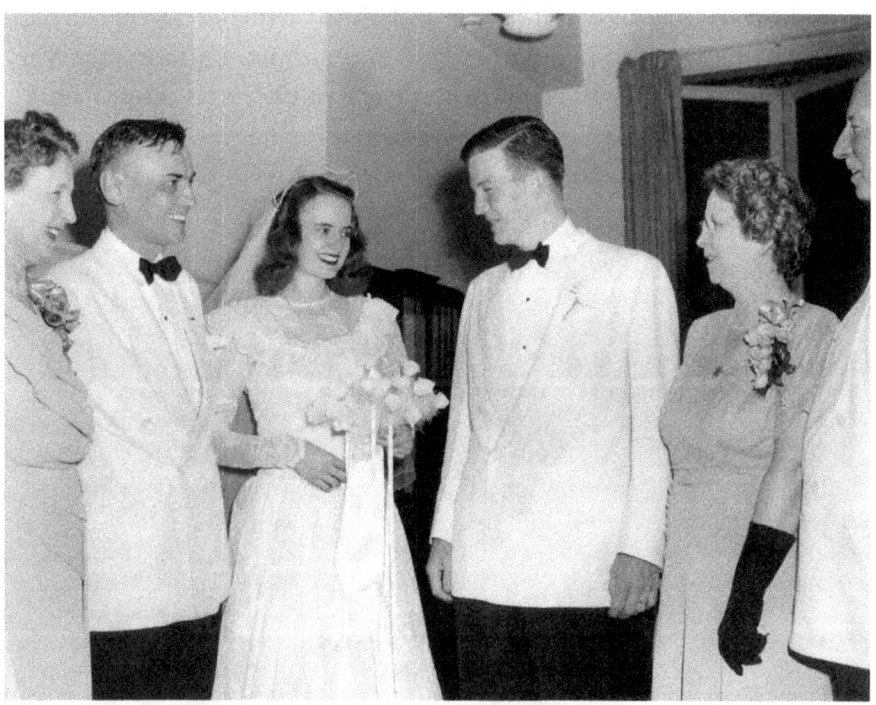

John and Mary Lou with parents

When I got back to Washington, the wedding plans were in full swing. Beautiful gifts started to pour in after the invitations were sent out. Appliances were still not readily available, so we received a lot of silver, crystal, china, and other gifts rather useless to a couple about to live in poverty. We got seven pairs of silver candlesticks. For the next few years, we gave silver candlesticks as wedding presents to our friends until we exhausted our supply. We also received numerous silver table cigarette lighters and holders. My grandfather gave us one hundred dollars as a gift, a princely sum at that time, and I bought my Lenox china with it.

Eight place settings! Now one setting costs twice that amount. John was horrified that I had spent the money that way, as he said we might not have any food to put on it. I still have the china and what food was on it is long since gone. However, when he arrived several days before the wedding, he and Mother really got into the spirit of opening gifts. "More loot," he would shout when a messenger delivered another package to the door. The two of them would rip off the paper and ooh and ah over the latest treasure.

I wanted to keep things reasonable and simple, so from the very beginning, I said I was only going to have two attendants. One

The champagne fountain

was my college roommate, Gloria, who was to wear her own wedding dress, which looked well with mine and did not have a train. She would carry red roses, while I carried white. The second was the young daughter of a family friend, Margaret Brown, who was to be flower girl. Her mother made her a long organdy dress. John could not contain himself when picking his attendants. He immediately chose his childhood friend, Ted Fordney, as best

THE WEDDING

man, then he invited almost everyone at Yale to be ushers. It was a male-dominated wedding. They all showed up in their appropriate tuxedos, so our guests were very efficiently seated. By then, Gloria was married to her husband Dick. They very kindly took charge of our luggage, so it would not be sabotaged by the huge crew of Yale pranksters, and got it to our room in the same hotel the reception was to be held in. No one knew this secret location except Gloria, Dick, and my parents. They also hid John's car near the hotel.

Dick had another duty, at the bachelor party the night before the wedding. This party was a dreadful custom still in vogue at that time. John had a large and enthusiastic crowd of bachelors to celebrate the death knell of his freedom with him, but Dick got him safely home to his parents in their hotel suite not too much the worse for wear. At the last minute, his childhood friends, Pat and Bo Johnson, who by then had one child, were able to come to the wedding from Lake Bluff. Bo joined the tribe of ushers.

The day of our wedding dawned bright and steamy hot as only Washington can be in the summertime. I was a nervous bride, and my mother was worse. If possible, my father was the worst of all. In mid-morning, our dear best man Ted called to inform me he had left his pants out in Virginia at his old family home, and he had no transportation to go and get them. Also, he had picked up his white tuxedo jacket and it had a big catsup stain on it. What should he do? He was laying this at the feet of the bride??? We had gotten to be good friends during the waiting period after I was engaged. He was going to college in Washington and would occasionally take me out for a beer to relieve my complete boredom, stuck in the house like a nun with my parents after my former freewheeling lifestyle. Thus, he felt it was OK for him to come to me with his little problems. I told him to kindly work it out for himself. I may have offered some advice on how to get the catsup off of his jacket. I had several more reports from him during the day. He finally rounded up his brother Ben to drive the pants in from Virginia. On the way from rural Virginia with this essential part of our wedding, the best man's pants, an airliner crashed right next to the highway he was driving on. He helped rescue some of the people, I think. The whole story remains a bit fuzzy to me, but Ted did show up at the wedding in pants.

Like most brides, I do not remember much about our actual wedding. It was very hot, and my veil was sticky on my face. The little chapel was overflowing, and I am sure the guests were relieved to get to the air-conditioned reception. There they were served little sandwiches, odds and ends of canapés, and the wedding cake. The champagne came out of a flowing fountain, which we all thought was remarkable, particularly the groom, who was a bit dazed by the whole day.

♥

Chapter Fifteen

The Honeymoon

OUR PLANS WERE TO LEAVE the next day to drive through New England and across Canada in the Red Cadillac. We would spend the summer with John's parents in Lake Bluff until it was time to go back to school on the GI Bill. John had a little money saved for summer spending money, as there would not be time for him to get a job. We would eat and sleep on the largesse of his parents. The day after our wedding, we decided we would stop and tell my parents goodbye and thank them for the wedding.

We also had two small problems. I had developed a sharp pain in my side that we were afraid might be appendicitis, and all of John's clothes in the trunk of his car had gotten wet in a rainstorm when his trunk leaked. He was not aware of it until we started sorting our luggage out. When we got to our apartment, Mother and Dad were packing to leave for New Haven for Lewis' master's degree ceremony. When they heard about our problems, they suggested that we stay in their apartment for a few days while they were gone. They were making some business side trips and would not be back for about a week. We could wash and clean John's clothes, and I could go to a doctor to find out what was causing the pain. There was a grocery store downstairs; as an extra gift to us, we could charge our groceries there. We accepted this kind offer. We were both worn out anyway, and there was no big hurry to get to Lake Bluff. They gave us one bedroom that night and left the next morning for New Haven. Thus, we spent the second night of our marriage with my parents.

The morning Mother and Dad left, Pat and Bo Johnson called the apartment to tell them goodbye. They were heading back to Chicago. They were quite amazed when John answered the phone. They had seen a little of Washington but were fast running out of money. After a brief consultation with me, John suggested they come to the apartment and stay another day or so and finish seeing the city. They had married right after the war and had not had a honeymoon, so this was their first real trip away from their growing family, which would eventually number six. They could have free room and board with us, thanks to the generosity of my innocent parents. We all thought that this sounded like great fun, so they hopped on a bus and arrived a short time later. Meanwhile, they told Ted about it. They had shared his tiny digs up to this point. He felt that perhaps his duty as best man should be extended, so he also came. We gave Pat and Bo the bedroom with the twin beds, and Ted slept on the couch in the living room. He had not intended to stay overnight, but we were having so much fun, he could not bear to leave. This rather weird arrangement went on for three or four days with the Johnsons and us sightseeing during the day and enjoying delicious steaks and other goodies at night. Ted came and went, having to attend his classes at George Washington. The second day he arrived with a glorious little Victorian book advising brides on what to expect when they got married that he had found in an antique bookstore. He entertained us by reading aloud from it in the evenings. After our guests finally departed, we headed up into New England on our official honeymoon, leaving the grocery bill behind for my parents as the last souvenir of their spoiled daughter.

We traveled in the Red Cadillac up through Maine, where I had my first taste of French-fried clams. As our money dwindled, we headed for the Honeymoon—Lake Bluff via Canada. When

THE HONEYMOON

we crossed into Canada and they asked each of us where we were born, John answered "Jacksonville, Florida." He was really born in Lakeland, Florida, but I think he was still slightly dazed at joining the ranks of married men.

When we arrived in Lake Bluff, we were warmly welcomed by John's family. The household had expanded since our last visit at Easter. His sister Ruth, fourteen years older than he, her husband Decker, and their baby son Fred had moved into the big house. Deck was an engineer temporarily assigned to a job building a power plant in the Chicago area. They could not find a house to rent for this short period, so Mother and Dad Walbridge urged them to join the crowd in their house. I fell in love with Ruth instantly, and have remained devoted to her all the years she has been my sister-in-law. We were assigned a bedroom with an appropriate double bed for a newly married couple. We shared the bathroom with Ruth and her family, but no one was used to numerous bathrooms in those days, so that did not seem like a hardship. I met the rest of the immediate family shortly after—John's brother Bud, his wife, Billie (Emma), and their four children ranging in age from seven to eleven. They lived in Libertyville, about seven or eight miles west of Lake Bluff, but I soon found I would see them frequently.

I settled in to learn a few domestic skills from my new family. Ruth and Grandmere—the name the grandchildren called John's mother—did most of the cooking but allowed me to make a salad or whatever menial task they thought I was capable of. They were very encouraging and never criticized anything I attempted. We all ate together every night in the summer dining room, a big glassed-in porch. After dinner, Dad Walbridge and I did the dishes. He washed, and I dried and put away. We had many long talks while doing this. Meanwhile, John happily rediscovered his boyhood friends who were still living in the area or who were home for the summer before going back to school. Together, they pursued those then-masculine sports of softball, golf, and boating. While he was doing these enjoyable activities, I was supposed to be writing the three hundred or so thank-you notes for our wedding gifts, spurred on by my mother-in-law, my sister-in-law, and my Aunt Betty. These letters were written on little engraved notecards that said "Mrs. John Tuthill Walbridge, Jr." on the front. In that chauvinistic society, the bridegroom did not help with this boring task as they do today. Usually, if it was a nice day, Betty and I with her children would go to the beach, and I would slave away there lying in the sand. I suppose some of the notes went out with a few grains of Lake Michigan sand. It took me all summer to do it, and I hated every minute of it.

After a few weeks of this program of bidding my new husband fond farewell while he went off to his daytime golf match or his evening softball game, I became a bit restless. I was used to being pampered by all of those nice Southern men, and here I was spending my evenings with my parents-in-law instead of my parents. On weekends, the program varied slightly. John usually played golf with his brother-in-law Deck, and occasionally his father, instead of his chums. I was invited to come watch the evening softball games, but the other girls there sat and talked about things I did not know anything about and did not exactly welcome me warmly into their close-knit little group. The last straw was when one of his friends bought an old ninety-foot yacht in Sturgeon Bay and asked John to help bring it back to Waukegan. My Navy man was delighted to join the crew and gave me a hasty farewell kiss as he shouldered his duffle bag and left without a backward glance at his new bride. That night while doing the dishes, Dad Walbridge and I had a long talk—tearful on my part. I pointed out to him that obviously John had made a big mistake getting married, as he did not seem very interested in spending time with me other than in bed. Dad reassured me that he was positive it was nothing personal. It just took a bit of time for a man to get used to being married. Women adjusted better than men did, as it was in their nature to settle into the domestic state. However, he certainly could see my point. When John returned from his cruise, which was an adventure he will have to tell you about, Dad Walbridge took him aside and had a little talk with him. The gist of it was that he should give up softball or golf and

THE HONEYMOON

avoid life-threatening cruises in the future if he wanted to remain in the state "Wedded Bliss." John, being basically a kind and agreeable man, went along with his father's suggestion and selected softball as his sacrifice, being least enthused about that particular sport.

Soon, his friends, male and female, accepted me into their group, and we started going out in the evenings, as we had when he was wooing me away from my Southern boyfriends. Our recreation consisted of going to the movies and then out to the little roadhouses where I had gone with him on our first dates. After an evening of dancing and sipping on a few beers or Cokes at one of those hot, dusty places, our favorite finish to the evening was to climb over the fence of the exclusive Knollwood Country Club and take a dip in the pool. Obviously, we still had not quite grown up, even though we were married. We could have gone to the beach for a swim, but it was much more fun to slip silently into the water and swim without splashing and alerting the night watchman.

That summer I was introduced to a Walbridge birthday custom that I soon found very tedious. Every family birthday, which all seemed to occur in the summer, was celebrated on the closest Sunday. Interspersed with these birthday gatherings were family get-togethers of the extended family. Besides John's brother Bud and his family, there were numerous other aunts, uncles, cousins, etc., etc. There was Dad's oldest sister Aunt Nora and her two daughters, husbands, and little children. Then there were Uncle Bob and Aunt Clara from Milwaukee. She was the mega-cook of the family, a superb master of cakes, potato salad, and homemade bread. Then there was Uncle Charles and Aunt Blanche with their two daughters from Park Ridge. Another sister, Aunt Dolly from Kalamazoo, showed up occasionally, and I especially loved her. We had lots of common interests including clothes and antiques. And, as a grand finale, there was Aunt Mary Lou, her husband, and five or six kids. All were gentle, loving people without a mean bone in any of their bodies. They all thought I was threateningly thin and happily stuffed me with the contributions they brought to the picnics. These gatherings were always at our house; like my grandfather in Fayetteville, Dad Walbridge was the patriarch. Mother Walbridge had one nephew . . .

♥

Epilogue

The Next Sixty-Four Years

AND THAT IS HOW OUR MOTHER'S NARRATIVE ends, in the middle of a sentence, as though she had walked out of the room still talking, as she is still wont to do. The rest of her story, which she did not see fit to write, can be told simply here.

In the fall of 1947 John returned to Yale as a senior, changing his major from electrical engineering to business. That winter they lived in a chilly cottage by Long Island Sound. While John did his last classes, Mary Lou earned some extra money as an inept office worker (and occasionally wrote his papers). She did eventually learn to type, although always erratically. When John graduated, they went back to Illinois, moving into a tiny apartment in Bud and Billy's farmhouse outside Libertyville. By the end of the next summer Mary Lou was pregnant, ready to make her first contribution to the Baby Boom. John began trying to establish himself in business. When the baby was born (John III, in accordance with the Walbridge tradition of unimaginative onomastics), they had a little laundry in Libertyville. In 1953 Mary was born. ("Mary is a grand old name," John insisted as Mary Lou pushed.) By then John had a cabinet manufacturing company, and they were living in a little house in Libertyville that her father and mother had bought to retire in.

When the cabinet business ran into difficulty, John took a job managing a fence company in Escanaba, Michigan, so in the summer of 1956 Mary Lou found herself in an old house with bad sewers in the Upper Peninsula of Michigan. There she lived for sixteen years while John ran and then bought the fence company. The fence company turned into a cedar home company, never quite prosperous but always interesting. Mary Lou, once a Washington belle, found herself an Upper Peninsula lady, ensnared by the grim charms of that harsh and beautiful land.

Mary Lou and her house by the river, winter (as usual), 1976

When the children were old enough to have lunch at school, she began working for the company, resurrecting her shaky secretarial skills. Officially, her job was pricing house packages, but, though no one ever called her that, she had become an architect, transforming the dreamy sketches of customers into workable house plans. Eventually she designed her own home, a beautiful rambling home on a wooded bluff above the Escanaba River. She and John lived there for thirty years, as the business bounced along uncertainly, the children grew up, went away, became educated, came back, married, and made their own lives. John III became a professor, Mary an obstetrician, and grandchildren, and then great-grandchildren came.

At long last, the business was sold. The house on the river with its quarter-mile driveway, part of which we children once used as a toboggan run, was no longer practical, so she and John moved into a somewhat smaller home, a little closer to town, but still in the woods. Eventually, they also acquired a little condo on Jekyll Island off the Georgia coast where they now spend the winter.

As we write this, that is Mary Lou's life. She is turning eighty-seven now and walks with a cane. She still cooks, superbly: her days of being good for nothing but salad and dishwashing are six decades in the past. (John learned not to criticize after she threw a badly cooked hamburger at him early in their marriage.) In the fall they move to Georgia, and in April they return to the Upper Peninsula.

John Walbridge is bent now, rather deaf, and somewhat prone to falling asleep in his chair if he is not wearing his hearing aids. But when Mary Lou looks at him, she still sees the handsome and dashing young man who snatched her away from his rivals more than half a century ago.

♥

John and Mary Lou
on their 60th wedding anniversary

EPILOGUE

Appendix

A Sixtieth Anniversary Toast

THE FOLLOWING IS A TOAST given by John Walbridge III at Mary Lou and John's sixtieth anniversary party.

We are gathered to celebrate the sixtieth wedding anniversary of John Walbridge, Jr., and Mary Lou Walbridge. The morning we chistened their first great-grandchild, Elizabeth Victoria Walbridge, variously known as "Evey" and "the Princess Elizabeth."

Sixty years is a long time for a marriage nowadays. When they were married in another century, the country was full of young veterans of World War II. The country was run by people who had served in World War I, and there were still a handful of veterans of the Civil War. Harry Truman was president. Rock and Roll hadn't been invented. TV was just getting started. George W. Bush was already known, though only as the Yale baseball team captain's baby.

A lot has happened since. There have been four more wars, and ten new presidents. My father has moved from an Eisenhower Republican to somewhere just to the right of Hugo Chavez.

A TOAST

My parents eventually got a television, though not until 1968, to the deep annoyance of my sister and me. There are computers and the internet. My parents moved into the northern wilderness and have stayed there for fifty years. There have been children, graduations, weddings, grandchildren, more graduations and weddings, and finally a great-grandchild.

But my mother is still beautiful, my father is still handsome, and my parents are still married.

On the other hand, sixty years is just a link in a longer chain. Last night we watched a program of family pictures that my sister Mary put together. There were many people who are no longer with us:

My grandparents, John Tuthill Walbridge, Sr., and Mabel Walbridge, whom we now know to have really been named Amiable, and Vance and Madge Sailor,

My Uncle Bud and Aunt Billy,

My mother's brother Lewis,

My first wife Linda,

and too many friends to mention, some of whose family are here tonight.

But my parents are a strong link in the chain binding seven generations together, from their own proud great-grandparents to their first great-grandchild.

So I would like to offer a toast to John and Mary Lou Walbridge, and may we all meet again in 2017 to celebrate their 70th anniversary.

♥

About the Author

Mary Lou Walbridge was born in Missouri in 1924 and grew up in Arkansas and Missouri. She graduated from Syracuse University in 1946. In 1947 she married John Walbridge and eventually settled in the Upper Peninsula of Michigan, where she and her husband owned a lumber business for half a century, during which time she designed hundreds of houses. She is now retired and divides her time between Gladstone in the Upper Peninsula and Jekyll Island, Georgia. She has two children, two grandsons, several step-grandchildren, and four great-grandchildren. This is her first book.

www.ingramcontent.com/pod-product-compliance
Lightning Source LLC
Chambersburg PA
CBHW071703040426
42446CB00011B/1899